Commitment
in the
Workplace

Advanced Topics in Organizational Behavior

The **Advanced Topics in Organizational Behavior** series examines current and emerging issues in the field of organizational behavior. Written by researchers who are widely acknowledged subject area experts, the books provide an authoritative, up-to-date review of the conceptual, research, and practical implications of the major issues in organizational behavior.

Commitment
in the
Workplace
Theory,
Research,
and
Application

John P. Meyer
Natalie J. Allen

Advanced Topics in
Organizational Behavior ATOB

SAGE Publications
International Educational and Professional Publisher
Thousand Oaks   London   New Delhi

For information, address to:

SAGE Publications, Inc.
2455 Teller Road
Thousand Oaks, California 91320
E-mail: order@sagepub.com

SAGE Publications Ltd.
6 Bonhill Street
London EC2A 4PU
United Kingdom

SAGE Publications India Pvt. Ltd.
M-32 Market
Greater Kailash I
New Delhi 110 048 India

Printed in the United States of America

Library of Congress Cataloging-in-Publication Data

Meyer, John P., 1950-
    Commitment in the workplace: Theory, research, and application /
John P. Meyer and Natalie J. Allen.
       p. cm.
    Includes bibliographical references and index.
    ISBN 0-7619-0104-3 (acid-free paper). —ISBN 0-7619-0105-1
(pbk.: acid-free paper)
    1. Employee motivation. 2. Employee morale. 3. Work ethic.
4. Organizational behavior. I. Allen, Natalie Jean. II. Title.
III. Series.
HF5549.5.M63M49 1997   96-45780
658.3'14—dc20

09 08 07 06 05 12 11 10 9 8

Acquiring Editor:	Marquita Flemming
Editorial Assistant:	Frances Borghi
Production Editor:	Sherrise M. Purdum
Production Assistant:	Karen Wiley
Typesetter/Designer:	Marion S. Warren
Print Buyer:	Anna Chin

Contents

To our families

Preface

We started to conduct research on commitment in the early 1980s. Our interest was stimulated initially by practical considerations: What made some volunteers in nonprofit organizations so highly committed to their work, and how might this sense of commitment be instilled in others? As we began to examine the literature for clues about how commitment develops and is maintained, we discovered little consensus on the meaning of commitment. We spent many hours discussing the various definitions and trying to determine who was "right." Eventually, we came to the conclusion that commitment is a multifaceted construct and that our understanding of how people become committed to an organization, nonprofit or otherwise, is better served by acknowledging this complexity rather than by choosing one approach over another.

Our main objective in writing this book was to summarize what we have learned over the last decade and a half about what commitment is, how it develops, and what its implications are both for employees and for their organizations. Our focus is largely on the results of quantitative empirical research undertaken to establish *general principles* that apply across organizations (at least in North America). We recognize, therefore, that our treatment of the topic might have most obvious relevance to an academic audience, whether they are actively involved in commitment research or have a general interest in organizational behavior research.

It is our hope, however, that those with more practical interests will also benefit from reading this book. Indeed, we believe that the framework provided here will help provide a better understanding of the commitment process and allow practitioners to scrutinize carefully the reports of more in-depth qualitative analyses of what did or did not work in other organizations and to evaluate what programs are most likely to work for them. Our *scientific* approach, therefore, should complement the treatment provided in business and trade journals, as well as in the popular press.

The title of this book, *Commitment in the Workplace,* was chosen to reflect the various entities within the world of work to which one might become committed, including the organization, job, profession/occupation, manager/supervisor, team, and union. Indeed, it is becoming increasingly apparent that to explain why people do what they do at work, we need to understand the potentially complex relations among their various work and nonwork commitments. Nevertheless, the reader will discover that much of the theory and research discussed in this book focuses on employees' commitment to the organization. This focus reflects the state of the field: Only recently have researchers begun to look systematically at other work-relevant commitments. We attempt, at various points throughout the book, to demonstrate how what we have learned about *organizational commitment* might be applied to understanding commitment to other entities.

Some might question whether employee commitment is a relevant issue in this era of rapid change, including reengineering and downsizing. The comment made by one executive upon learning that we were involved in this project was, "I guess it will be a short book." We acknowledge that relationships between organizations and their employees are indeed changing. This fact, however, does not undermine the value of understanding how commitments develop and influence the nature of employee-organization relationships. To the contrary, we believe that workers, as human beings, inevitably develop commitments of one form or another that have an influence on their behavior at work. By understanding when and how commitments develop and how they help shape attitudes and behaviors, organizations will be in a better position to anticipate the impact that change will have and to manage it more effectively.

The contributions of many individuals and organizations over the years have helped shape our thinking, our research program, and ultimately, this book. These include the many theorists and investigators whose work we cite throughout this book, including those whose work we turned to when we first became interested in commitment, and the more recent contributors to the literature whose work has consistently helped renew our interest and clarify our understanding. Our own research was made possible by research grants from the Social Sciences and Humanities Research Council of Canada and Imperial Oil of Canada, Ltd. Several former graduate students—Ramona Bobocel, Ian Gellatly, Greg Irving, and Cathy Smith—were active contributors in our research program. We were also very fortunate to have a number of very capable research assistants—Denise McLean, Patricia Lee, Alanna Leffley, Linda Irving, Jeff Nolan, Meridith Black, and Julie McCarthy—who spent many hours in the library and at the computer. Meridith and Julie also assisted greatly in the preparation of the final manuscript (and its previous incarnations). To each of these individuals we owe a sincere debt of gratitude. We also thank Julian Barling and Kevin Kelloway, the series editors, for inviting us to write this book, the reviewers for their helpful comments and suggestions, and Marquita Flemming and the editorial staff at Sage for their help in the production process. Finally, we thank our parents—Doug and Trudy Allen and Gerry and Toddy Meyer—for their early support and encouragement, and our families—Steve, Jeffrey, and Sarah Lupker, and Trudy, Matthew, and Samantha Meyer—for being there when we needed them the most. It is to you that we dedicate this book.

1

Introduction

*The old notion of corporate allegiance has faded. Maybe that's not such a
bad thing.* ("A Question of Loyalty," 1991, p. 8)

*Loyalty is by no means dead. It remains one of the great engines of
business success.* (Reichheld, 1996, p. 1)

These comments reflect quite different perceptions of the relationships today's
workers have with their organizations and of the implications of these
relationships. As is often the case when one encounters such widely different points
of view, the answer probably lies somewhere in the middle, and the disagreement
results from differences in perspective. To discover the "truth" (or at least to
identify the basis for disagreement), we need to examine clearly what we mean by
such terms as *allegiance* and *loyalty*. We also need to consider carefully what the
potential benefits or costs of attachment might be and to determine systematically
whether those benefits or costs are realized.

1

This book is about commitment in the workplace and is intended to address questions concerning workers' relationships with their organizations (among other things), how those relationships are established, and how they influence workers' behavior, well-being, and contributions to organizational effectiveness. These are important issues, as evidenced by the amount of attention they have received in the academic literature, in business and trade journals, and in the popular press. We have been involved for more than a dozen years in the study of commitment. Our objective in writing this book was to summarize the findings of our work and that of scores of other researchers in such a way that the findings can be evaluated for both their scientific merit and their practical value. Much has been learned over the years through the scientific study of commitment in the workplace. We hope that, in presenting the results of this research, we provide some insight to those whose primary interest is in application. Admittedly, however, many questions are yet to be answered. Therefore, we also hope that our review of existing research and our suggestions for future directions will provide some guidance to those who are or will be involved in the study of commitment.

Our main emphasis in this book is on employees' commitment to the organization, referred to in the academic literature as *organizational commitment*. Many other commitments that people develop are important in understanding their behavior in the workplace, however. These include commitment to the work group, manager, occupation, profession, career, and union. A case can also be made that commitments outside work, in addition to being of interest in their own right, have an influence on behavior at work. Space does not permit us to do justice to all the research that has been conducted in these areas. Our focus on organizational commitment derives, in part, from our own research interests. Moreover, Morrow and McElroy (1993, p. 1), editors of the special issue of the *Journal of Business Research* devoted to workplace commitment, noted that "organizational commitment is the most maturely developed of the work commitment family of constructs." Consequently, much of what has been learned about commitment to organizations can contribute to the understanding of other commitments.

Before we put commitment under the microscope, we first consider why it is important to do so. As we noted above, in addition to the scientific interest in the topic, much has been written in the popular press about employee commitment (or loyalty). This literature illustrates the concerns being raised by employers and employees themselves. By acknowledging these concerns, we begin to recognize the importance of finding answers.

What Is a Committed Employee?

Whether they are bemoaning the fact that employees are too committed (Whyte, 1956) or that commitment is a thing of the past (e.g., "The End of Corporate Loyalty," 1986), commentators typically describe the committed employee as one who stays with the organization through thick and thin, attends work regularly, puts in a full day (and maybe more), protects company assets, shares company goals, and so on. Viewed from an organizational perspective, having a committed workforce would clearly appear to be an advantage. But is there a downside? Randall (1987) suggested, for example, that a "blind" commitment to an organization can lead employees to accept the status quo even if it ultimately means that the company loses its ability to innovate and adapt to change. Others might argue that if gaining the loyalty of employees requires that employers reciprocate in kind, the cost might simply be too great; organizations cannot afford to guarantee employment.

What about the benefits and costs of commitment from the standpoint of the employee? Presumably, there are benefits to be derived from commitment. Why else would people allow themselves to become committed to anything? Organizations provide jobs to occupy time and money to pay bills, but it is unlikely that these incentives, in and of themselves, will create the kind of commitment that leads to the behavior described above. Perhaps the other things that organizations provide, such as the opportunity to do important and challenging work, to meet and interact with interesting people, and to learn new skills and develop as a person, lead to the development of commitment. If so, there would clearly seem to be advantages to working in an organization to which one can become committed. But there might be a downside to commitment for employees as well. For example, being committed to an organization might lead to the expenditure of time and energy that is therefore not available to invest elsewhere (e.g., family, hobbies). Moreover, those who are committed to an organization might be less concerned about developing knowledge and skills that would keep them marketable outside if the organization changed or ceased to exist.

It appears that, from the perspective of both the employer and the employee, commitment can have two faces. Unfortunately, it is relatively easy to paint either face, depending on the case one wants to make. To make an informed judgment about the benefits and cost of commitment, it is important to know how strong the connection is between employees' commitment and their willingness to "go to the wall" for the organization, as well as their tendency to blindly follow where the organization takes them (even if it is to the unemployment line). Similarly, it is important to understand the conditions that contribute to the development of commitment and the consequences of commitment from the employees' perspective. Do employees only become committed when doing so has a benefit, or can they be "trapped" into becoming committed (see Salancik, 1977b)? Are employees who are committed better or worse off than employees who are uncommitted? Are they happier, healthier, more satisfied with their careers? Do they suffer more when the organization undergoes change?

These important questions are all based on the premise that the stereotypical view of commitment is accurate, that commitment reflects loyalty and willingness to work toward organizational objectives. The term *commitment* has other meanings, however. Consider, for example, an employee who has been with the same company for more than 20 years, received several early promotions, but failed in several recent bids for promotion. It is clear to all that this individual's career has plateaued. Although the motivation that once existed is gone, the employee realizes that no other employer would be likely to provide him or her the same salary and benefits now being received. For all intents and purposes, this person is "committed" to remaining with the company, but it is unlikely that the consequences of this commitment will be the same as for the kind of commitment we discussed above. It is also important, therefore, that one understand the different forms that commitment can take, the conditions that lead to their development, and their implications for behavior.

Does Commitment Matter Anymore?

Much is being written about the fact that the world of work is changing (see Cascio, 1995). Included among the changes are increased global competition (Black, Gregersen, & Mendenhall, 1992), rapid developments in information technology (*Workplace of the Future,* 1993), reengineering of business (Hammer & Champy, 1993), and replacement of "jobs" with "roles" (Bridges, 1994). These changes are requiring new approaches to the way companies "organize." Much greater emphasis is being placed on flexibility and efficiency; companies must be able to adapt to changing conditions and to cut costs in order to be competitive. Many strategies used to achieve these objectives, including the introduction of new technology, consolidation of operations, and contracting out, involve the loss of jobs. Consequently, employees are being advised not to become too attached to their employers, but instead to look out for themselves and to ensure that they remain employable in the event of a layoff (e.g., Hirsch, 1987). It appears, then, that neither employers nor employees are or should be committed anymore.

Does this mean the study of commitment is outdated as well? We do not think so, and for the following reasons. First, organizations are not disappearing; they may be becoming leaner, but they must maintain a core of people who *are* the organization. As organizations become smaller and jobs become more flexible, those who remain in the organization become even more important. Once the "fat" is gone, the remaining employees represent the "heart, brain, and muscle" of the organization. The jobs these employees will be doing are likely to be very different from those of their predecessors. For example, Bridges (1994) argued that the "job" as a fixed collection of tasks and responsibilities is disappearing and being replaced by broader "roles" that require a greater variety of skills and an ability to adapt to the demands of the situation. With the reduction of management and the flattening of the organizational hierarchy, employees are being given much more responsibility for decision making and for managing their own day-to-day activities. Therefore, it is all the more important that the organization be able to trust the employee to do what is right—something that commitment arguably ensures. Moreover, as new technology is introduced, many of the "simpler" tasks are being done by machines and computers. The tasks that remain for people require higher-level knowledge and skills. Training employees to perform these tasks will require substantial financial investment on the part of organizations, and once trained, these employees are likely to be highly marketable.

Second, organizations that contract out work to other companies or individuals will still be concerned about the commitment of these others. The organization's own success might depend on it. Admittedly, the commitment might be different, perhaps being of shorter duration and with a focus on a contract or project rather than on the organization itself. Thus, understanding how commitments develop and are maintained is important here as well.

Third, commitments develop naturally. There is reason to believe that people need to be committed to something; the opposite of commitment is alienation, and alienation is unhealthy (Kobasa, Maddi, & Kahn, 1982). If they become less committed to organizations, employees may channel their commitment in other directions (e.g., industry, careers, hobbies, volunteer groups). In addition to being of relevance to the understanding of the individual's own well-being, the behavioral consequences of these commitments might have implications for employees' relationships with their organizations. For example, employees who are reluctant to develop a commitment to an organization that cannot or will not reciprocate might instead become committed to their occupation/profession or to the industry in which they work. These employees might start to evaluate their skills and experience in terms of their marketability outside the organization, rather than by their implications for their current or future jobs in the organization ("The End of Corporate Loyalty," 1986). All things considered, then, understanding commitment and how it develops is as important now as it ever was.

Plan of the Book

As you have seen, there are many questions about what commitment is, how it affects behavior, how it develops, and what can be done to manage it effectively. Fortunately, a considerable amount of research has addressed these questions. Although we cannot discuss all of this research in detail, we provide a summary of what has been found and what it means. We begin in Chapter 2 with a discussion of the meaning of commitment. Here, we describe efforts to distinguish among different forms of commitment and the different constituencies within the organization to which these commitments are directed.

In Chapter 3, we discuss the consequences of commitment, and in Chapter 4, we look at how it develops. In these chapters, we place more emphasis on the scientific than on the practitioner literatures. Keep in mind, however, that the "laboratory" used in this research has been the workplace. The research reported in these chapters comes from observations, interviews, and surveys involving many thousands of employees in hundreds of organizations.

In Chapter 5, we discuss how specific organizational policies and practices (e.g., recruitment and selection, socialization and training, downsizing) affect employees' commitment to the organization. Again, our emphasis is on demonstrating links that have been established through empirical research. Throughout this chapter, we draw on the findings reported in Chapter 4 concerning the factors and processes involved in the development of commitment. Together, the two literatures provide a better understanding of how organizations can more effectively "manage for commitment."

In Chapter 6, we broaden our discussion of commitment beyond that to the organization. Specifically, we discuss how what we have learned about the multidimensional (or multifaceted) nature of commitment to the organization, its development, and its consequences can be applied to understanding commitment to other domains (e.g, occupation, profession, union). We also discuss how these different commitments might interact to influence behavior, career decisions, productivity, and so on.

In the concluding chapter, we provide an overview of what we have learned about commitment. We also identify what we consider to be some of the more important questions yet to be answered and suggest directions for future investigation.

2

Meaning of Commitment

---

n Chapter 1, we identified important questions that have been raised about employees' commitment to the organization: What are the costs and benefits for the organization of having a committed workforce? What are the costs and benefits of being committed for the employee? Is commitment in decline? Does commitment matter anymore? Before we can hope to answer these questions, we have to be clear about what we mean by commitment. Although we alluded in Chapter 1 to commitment as a complex construct, our objective here is to describe in more detail the different ways in which the term has been used and to illustrate how acknowledging the differences helps in sorting out some confusion that currently exists. This sets the stage for discussion of the development and consequences in subsequent chapters.

Recent efforts to clarify the meaning of commitment have taken two distinct directions. The first involves attempts to illustrate that commitment can take different forms; that is, the *nature* of the commitment that defines the relationship between an employee and some other entity (e.g., an organization) can vary. The second involves efforts to distinguish among the *entities* to which an employee becomes committed. These two approaches at classification are not incompatible, and although we first address each individually, we conclude this chapter with a discussion of how, in combination, the two approaches help clarify our understanding of commitment, how it develops, and its implications for individuals and organizations.

Before we discuss either of these recent approaches to classification, it is important that we acknowledge the more long-standing distinction that has been made between *attitudinal commitment* and *behavioral commitment* (Mowday, Porter, & Steers, 1982; Reichers, 1985; Salancik, 1977a; Scholl, 1981; Staw, 1977). This traditional distinction has had important implications not only for the definition and measurement of commitment but also for the approaches taken in the study of its development and consequences. Mowday et al. (p. 26) described these two approaches as follows:

> Attitudinal commitment focuses on the process by which people come to think about their relationship with the organization. In many ways it can be thought of as a mind set in which individuals consider the extent to which their own values and goals are congruent with those of the organization. . . . Behavioral commitment, on the other hand, relates to the process by which individuals become locked into a certain organization and how they deal with this problem.

The study of attitudinal commitment has typically involved the measurement of commitment (an attitude or mind-set), along with other variables presumed to be the antecedents to, or consequences of, commitment (e.g., Buchanan, 1974; Steers, 1977). The objectives of this research were to (a) demonstrate that strong commitment was associated with desirable outcomes (from an organizational perspective), such as lower absenteeism and turnover and higher productivity, and (b) determine what personal characteristics and situational conditions contributed to the development of high commitment. Although, implicitly, the aim was to establish causal connections, until recently most research in this tradition employed cross-sectional designs in which commitment and its antecedents and/or consequences were measured at the same time. At best, this kind of research allows us to establish whether relevant variables are related to one another (co-occur). Causality cannot be clearly established.

In the behavioral approach, employees were viewed as becoming committed to a particular course of action (e.g., maintaining employment with an organization), rather than to an entity. To the extent that an attitude (or mind-set) developed, this was considered to be a consequence of commitment to a course of action. For example, employees who are committed to remaining with their organizations might develop a more positive view of these organizations consistent with their behavior to avoid cognitive dissonance or to maintain positive self-perceptions (e.g., as being "in control" and doing what one "wants to do"). The objective in this research, therefore, was to discover the conditions under which an individual becomes committed to a course of action (Kiesler, 1971; Salancik, 1977a).

In the remainder of this chapter, we treat commitment as a *psychological state* but acknowledge that this state can develop retrospectively (as justification for an ongoing course of action) as proposed in the behavioral approach, as well as prospectively (e.g., based on perceptions of current or future conditions of work within an organization) as advocated in the attitudinal approach. We discuss the contributions that have been made by research in the behavioral tradition in our discussion of the development of commitment in Chapter 4. As an aside, however, work in the behavioral commitment tradition has important implications for other aspects of workplace commitment. Perhaps the most interesting of these is the escalation of commitment to a failing course of action. Decision makers who become committed to a decision have been shown to persist in a course of action (e.g., financial investments) despite objective evidence suggesting that it is not prudent to do so. (For a more detailed discussion of escalating commitment and its implications, see Brockner, 1992, and Staw & Ross, 1987.)

Nature of Commitment

In their review of the commitment literature, Mowday et al. (1982) observed little consensus on what the term *commitment* means. Rather, they noted that "researchers from various disciplines ascribed their own meanings to the topic, thereby increasing the difficulty involved in understanding the construct" (p. 20). In Table 2.1, we provide a sample of the various definitions that have been offered over the years. Although these definitions derive from the academic literature, our experience has been that the meaning varies as much or more in everyday use of the term (and related terms such as *allegiance, loyalty,* and *attachment*). Given the "flexibility" with which the term *commitment* is used, it is not surprising that opinion differs concerning whether it is good or bad, stable or in decline, and so on. From a scientific standpoint, we cannot begin to study the development and consequences of commitment systematically until the construct is defined and measures are developed. Similarly, practitioners will have difficulty taking guidance from the scientific literature, as well as from more popular treatments of the topic, until we clarify what we mean by commitment.

No definition in Table 2.1 is more "correct" or universally accepted than the others. The definitions are different, however, and it can only confuse the issue if we speak of commitment without indicating which definition we are using. Fortunately, the picture is not as confusing as it first appears. Meyer and Allen (1991) noted that the various definitions reflect three broad themes as indicated by the category labels in Table 2.1; that is, commitment has been viewed as reflecting an affective orientation toward the organization, a recognition of costs associated with leaving the organization, and a moral obligation to remain with the organization. To acknowledge that each of the three sets of definitions represents a legitimate but clearly different conceptualization of the commitment construct, Meyer and Allen proposed a three-component model of organizational commitment that we now describe in some detail.

A Three-Component Model of Commitment

Meyer and Allen (1991) noted that common to the various definitions of organizational commitment is "the view that commitment is a psychological state that (a) characterizes the employee's relationship with the organization, and (b) has implications for the decision to continue membership in the organization" (p. 67). Thus, regardless of the definition, "committed" employees are more likely to remain in the organization than are "uncommitted" employees. What differs across definitions—particularly definitions across categories in Table 2.1—is the nature of the psychological state being described. To acknowledge these differences, Meyer and Allen applied different labels to what they described as three *components* of commitment: affective, continuance, and normative.

> Affective commitment refers to the employee's emotional attachment to, identification with, and involvement in the organization. Employees with a strong affective commitment continue employment with the organization because they *want* to do so. Continuance commitment refers to an awareness of the costs associated with leaving the organization. Employees whose primary link to the organization is based on continuance commitment remain because they *need* to do so. Finally, normative commitment reflects a feeling of obligation to continue employment. Employees with a high level of normative commitment feel that they *ought* to remain with the organization. (p. 67)

TABLE 2.1 Definitions of Commitment

Affective Orientation

The attachment of an individual's fund of affectivity and emotion to the group. (Kanter, 1968, p. 507)

An attitude or an orientation toward the organization which links or attaches the identity of the person to the organization. (Sheldon, 1971, p. 143)

The process by which the goals of the organization and those of the individual become increasingly integrated or congruent. (Hall, Schneider, & Nygren, 1970, pp. 176-177)

A partisan, affective attachment to the goals and values of the organization, to one's role in relation to goals and values, and to the organization for its own sake, apart from its purely instrumental worth. (Buchanan, 1974, p. 533)

The relative strength of an individual's identification with and involvement in a particular organization. (Mowday, Porter, & Steers, 1982, p. 27)

Cost-Based

Profit associated with continued participation and a "cost" associated with leaving. (Kanter, 1968, p. 504)

Commitment comes into being when a person, by making a side bet, links extraneous interests with a consistent line of activity. (Becker, 1960, p. 32)

A structural phenomenon which occurs as a result of individual-organizational transactions and alterations in side bets or investments over time. (Hrebiniak & Alutto, 1972, p. 556)

Obligation or Moral Responsibility

Commitment behaviors are socially accepted behaviors that exceed formal and/or normative expectations relevant to the object of commitment. (Wiener & Gechman, 1977, p. 48)

The totality of internalized normative pressures to act in a way which meets organizational goals and interests. (Wiener, 1982, p. 421)

The committed employee considers it morally right to stay in the company, regardless of how much status enhancement or satisfaction the firm gives him or her over the years. (Marsh & Mannari, 1977, p. 59)

Meyer and Allen (1991) argued that it was more appropriate to consider affective, continuance, and normative commitment to be components, rather than types, of commitment because an employee's relationship with an organization might reflect varying degrees of all three. For example, one employee might feel both a strong attachment to an organization and a sense of obligation to remain. A second employee might enjoy working for the organization but also recognize that leaving would be very difficult from an economic standpoint. Finally, a third employee might experience a considerable degree of desire, need, and obligation to remain with the current employer. Consequently, researchers stand to gain a clearer understanding of an employee's relationship with an organization by considering the strength of all three forms of commitment together than by trying to classify it as being of a particular type.

As noted above, common to all conceptualizations of commitment is the notion that commitment binds an individual to the organization. Indeed, interest in organizational commitment derived in large measure from the belief that it was related to employee turnover. Considering the costs associated with turnover (Cascio, 1982), potentially much can be gained by finding ways to increase employees' commitment. Meyer and Allen (1991) noted, however, that focusing exclusively on turnover as a consequence of commitment is shortsighted; what employees do on the job is arguably as important as whether they stay or leave (cf. Meyer, Paunonen, Gellatly, Goffin, & Jackson, 1989). As we discuss in more detail in Chapter 3, the advantage of recognizing the existence of different forms of commitment is illustrated by findings of their differential association with such work-relevant behaviors as absenteeism, job performance, and citizenship behavior.

For reasons to be described below, the three-component conceptualization described here is used to guide our discussion of the development, consequences, and management of commitment in subsequent chapters. A description and brief discussion of measures developed to assess these three components is provided in the appendix. It is important, however, to acknowledge other approaches that have been developed recently in recognizing the multidimensional nature of commitment.

Other Classification Schemes

The classification system described above was derived from an effort to identify themes or commonalities in existing definitions of commitment. A somewhat different but not incompatible approach was taken by O'Reilly and his colleagues (Caldwell, Chatman, & O'Reilly, 1990; O'Reilly & Chatman, 1986; O'Reilly, Chatman, & Caldwell, 1991). Like Meyer and Allen (1991), they argued that commitment reflects the "psychological bond" that ties the employee to the organization but that the nature of the bond can differ. Following from Kelman's (1958) work on attitude and behavioral change, they argued that the psychological bond between an employee and an organization can take three distinct forms, which they labeled *compliance, identification,* and *internalization.*

> Compliance occurs when attitudes and behaviors are adopted not because of shared beliefs but simply to gain specific rewards. In this case, public and private attitudes may differ. Identification, in Kelman's terms, occurs when an individual accepts influence to establish or maintain a satisfying relationship; that is, an individual may feel proud to be a part of a group, respecting its values and accomplishments without adopting them as his or her own. Internalization occurs when influence is accepted because the induced attitudes and behavior are congruent with one's own values; that is, the values of the individual and the group or organization are the same. (O'Reilly & Chatman, 1986, p. 493)

O'Reilly and Chatman (1986) proposed that an employee's psychological attachment to an organization can reflect varying combinations of these three psychological foundations. Like Meyer and Allen (1991), they noted that the behavioral consequences of the various forms of commitment might be quite different. To illustrate, they examined relations between measures of compliance, identification, and internalization and several outcome measures (e.g., prosocial behavior, turnover intention, turnover). Identification and internalization were negatively related to turnover intention and turnover and positively related to prosocial behavior. Moreover, in some analyses, it was found that identification and internalization each accounted for unique variance in the outcome measures (each contributed uniquely to prediction). Compliance showed the opposite pattern of relations and was also found to contribute uniquely to the prediction of turnover intention.

Although it served to sensitize researchers to the multidimensional nature of commitment, the impact of O'Reilly's classification system has been weakened by the difficulty of distinguishing identification and internalization (e.g., Caldwell et al., 1990; O'Reilly et al., 1991; Vandenberg, Self, & Seo, 1994); the measures tend to correlate highly with one another and to show similar patterns of correlations with measures of other variables (for exceptions, see Becker, Billings, Eveleth, & Gilbert, 1996, and Harris, Hirschfeld, Feild, & Mossholder, 1993). In fact, in their more recent research (Caldwell et al., 1990; O'Reilly et al., 1991), O'Reilly and his colleagues combined the identification and internalization items to form a measure of what they called *normative commitment.* (Notice that this construct corresponds more closely to affective commitment in Meyer and Allen's [1991] model and should not be confused with the latter's use of the term *normative commitment.*) Furthermore, although compliance (also referred to as *instrumental commitment* in more recent work) is clearly distinct from identification and internalization, one might question whether it can truly be considered commitment. Not only is it distinct from other common definitions of commitment (see Table 2.1), but it is also considered by some to be the antithesis of commitment. Scholl (1981), for example, argued that commitment serves to maintain behavior in the absence of reward. Finally, compliance has been found to correlate positively with employee turnover (O'Reilly & Chatman, 1986), whereas commitment is generally assumed to reduce turnover (Mowday et al., 1982). To include compliance as a basis for commitment, therefore, invites confusion.

One approach to reconciling O'Reilly and colleagues' classification scheme (with the exception of compliance) with that of Meyer and Allen (1991) is suggested by the former's use of the term *bases* of commitment. Identification and internalization might best be considered mechanisms by which commitment— particularly affective commitment—develops; that is, employees' affective attachment to their organizations might be *based on* a desire to establish a rewarding relationship with an organization (identification) and/or on congruence in the goals and values held by the individual and the organization (internalization). We discuss this possibility in greater detail in Chapter 4.

Before discussing the focus of commitment, we note that several other attempts have been made to identify and measure different forms of commitment (e.g., Angle & Perry, 1981; Jaros, Jermier, Koehler, & Sincich, 1993; Mayer & Schoorman, 1992; Penley & Gould, 1988). These approaches have both similarities and differences, which, unfortunately, space does not permit us to describe in detail. An important goal for future research is to develop a more unified approach to the classification and measurement of commitment. In the meantime, however, it is critical that those conducting research and those intending to apply the findings be aware of differences in the conceptualization and measurement of commitment. One potential source of confusion is the fact that, in some cases, different labels are used to describe very similar constructs (e.g., calculative commitment and continuance commitment), whereas in others, the same labels are used to describe different constructs (e.g., normative commitment as described by Caldwell et al., 1990, and Allen & Meyer, 1990a). Moreover, the instruments used to measure commitment sometimes do not correspond to the construct as defined or conceptualized in the development of hypotheses (see Cohen & Lowenberg, 1990, and Meyer & Allen, 1984, for a more detailed discussion and examples). It is incumbent upon researchers, therefore, to be explicit in their definitions and to use appropriate instruments. Consumers of this research should attend to these definitions and measures in drawing inferences from the data, rather than rely solely on the labels that are attached to the constructs.

In summary, the growing consensus among commitment theorists and researchers is that commitment is a multidimensional construct. They exhibit less agreement about what the various dimensions are. For present purposes, we use Meyer and Allen's (1991) three-component model as the basis for our discussion of the development and implications of commitment. Of the multidimensional models identified here, this model and the measures associated with it have undergone the most extensive empirical evaluation to date (see Allen & Meyer, 1996, for a review). Moreover, because Meyer and Allen's model was developed from an identification of common themes in the conceptualization of commitment from the existing literature, using this model allows us to incorporate the results of a broad array of studies using measures other than those developed specifically for purposes of testing the model. Most important, the many studies that have used the Organizational Commitment Questionnaire (Mowday, Steers, & Porter, 1979) can be included in our discussion of affective commitment. This is also true of research using O'Reilly and Chatman's (1986) identification and internalization measures.

Focus of Commitment

When we say that someone is committed, we usually imply or state specifically that he or she is committed to something (e.g., he is committed to his family; she is committed to the project). Within the organizational behavior literature, much of the theoretical work on commitment has focused on commitment to the organization. This emphasis has raised two broad concerns. First, Morrow (1983) noted that "organizational commitment" as a construct was potentially redundant with other work commitment constructs such as job involvement (Kanungo, 1982; Lodahl & Kejner, 1965), work ethic (Blood, 1969; Buchholz, 1976; Mirels & Garrett, 1971), and career commitment (Blau, 1985; Greenhaus, 1971). For example, the variables identified as potential antecedents of organizational commitment, as well as those identified as consequences, were not unlike the antecedents and consequences of these other work commitment variables. Morrow argued that, to warrant status as a variable worthy of study for its own sake, a commitment construct must be shown to be distinguishable from related constructs and to make a unique contribution to the understanding of important outcome variables (e.g., turnover, job performance).

Fortunately, recent research findings provide a strong case for the continued study of the organizational commitment construct. For example, organizational commitment has been shown in factor analytic studies to be distinguishable from job satisfaction, job involvement, career salience, occupational commitment, turnover intention, work group attachment, and the Protestant work ethic (Brooke, Russell, & Price, 1988; Cohen, 1993b; Mathieu & Farr, 1991; Meyer, Allen, & Smith, 1993; Morrow & McElroy, 1986; Mueller, Wallace, & Price, 1992; Randall & Cote, 1991). Moreover, organizational commitment has also been found to relate differently from these other attitude and commitment constructs to variables presumed to be their antecedents (Brooke et al., 1988; Mathieu & Farr, 1991; Meyer et al., 1993). Finally, and perhaps most important, commitment to the organization has been shown to contribute uniquely to the prediction of important outcome variables (e.g., Blau & Boal, 1989; Meyer et al., 1993; Tett & Meyer, 1993). In the light of these and related findings, Morrow (1993) concluded in her recent review of the literature that although organizational commitment is itself a multidimensional construct, it is clearly distinguishable from other forms of workplace commitment and therefore worthy of study for its own sake.

The second concern was raised by Reichers (1985). She noted that, in the organizational commitment literature, the organization "typically is viewed as a monolithic, undifferentiated entity that elicits an identification and attachment on the part of the individual" (p. 469). In reality, however, she argued that organizations comprise various "coalitions and constituencies" (e.g., owners/managers; rank-and-file employees, customers/clients), each with its own goals and values that may or may not be compatible with the goals of the organizations themselves. Therefore, organizational commitment can be best understood as a collection of multiple commitments. This view raises the possibility that (a) employees can have varying commitment profiles and that (b) conflict can exist among an employee's commitments.

Reichers (1986) tested her multiple-constituency framework by assessing commitment to the organization in general, using the Organizational Commitment Questionnaire, and to four constituencies of relevance to 124 mental health professionals (top management, funding agencies, clients and larger public, and professional goals and standards). She found that commitment to the organization correlated significantly only with commitment to top management's goals and values. Not surprisingly, therefore, these mental health professionals were less committed to the organization when they believed that their own pattern of commitments to the various constituencies differed from that of top management.

Becker (1992) provided additional support for the multiple-constituency approach by demonstrating that employees' commitments to top management, supervisor, and work groups contributed significantly beyond commitment to the organization in the prediction of job satisfaction, intention to quit, and prosocial organizational behavior. On the basis of a reanalysis of Becker's data, however, Hunt and Morgan (1994) suggested that commitment to specific constituencies might be better viewed as exerting their influence on these outcome variables indirectly through their influence on overall commitment to the organization; that is, commitment to each constituency contributes to employees' overall commitment to the organization, which in turn influences the various outcome measures. Nevertheless, Hunt and Morgan also noted that this mediating effect might be strongest for constituencies psychologically closer to the organization (e.g., top management, supervisor) and that direct effects of commitment to constituencies might be expected for outcomes of more direct relevance to that constituency.

In yet another analysis of these data, Becker and Billings (1993) used cluster analysis to identify commitment profiles (differing patterns of commitment to the various constituencies within the organization). They found four dominant profiles:

> (1) the Locally Committed (employees who are attached to their supervisor and work group), (2) the Globally Committed (who are attached to top management and the organization), (3) the Committed (who are attached to both local and global foci), and (4) the Uncommitted (who are attached to neither local nor global foci). (p. 177)

Employees who were committed to both local and global foci had the highest level of overall job satisfaction, were least likely to intend to leave, and demonstrated the highest levels of prosocial behavior. The locally and globally committed employees did not differ from one another in terms of general attitudes and behavior, falling between the committed and uncommitted in all cases. Interestingly, however, when attitudes and prosocial behavior directed at the supervisor and work group were assessed, both were found to be higher among the locally committed than among the globally committed. Again, this finding suggests that relations between commitment to specific constituencies and behavior will be strongest when constituency-relevant behavior is examined.

More recently, Becker et al. (1996) measured newcomers' commitment to both the organization and their immediate supervisors and related these measures to supervisor ratings of job performance. Separate measures of commitment—one based on internalization and the other on identification—were obtained for both foci—supervisor and organization. Becker et al. found that commitment to the supervisor—particularly commitment based on internalization of supervisor values—was more strongly related to performance ratings than was commitment to the organization. Although the performance measures obtained in this study (e.g., quantity and quality of work) were clearly relevant to the organization, the stronger correlation with supervisor commitment might suggest that supervisors' evaluations of performance were particularly sensitive to aspects of performance that were relevant to their own objectives. This suggestion might have made the criteria somewhat more constituency-specific. At any rate, the findings provide additional evidence to suggest that commitment to constituencies within the organization can have important implications for organization-relevant behavior.

Like Reichers (1985), Lawler (1992) noted that organizations are composed of multiple subgroups, or collectives, and that employees can develop commitments to one or more of these. One additional contribution made by Lawler, however, is the idea that these collectives are sometimes "nested," meaning that belonging to one requires belonging to another. For example, being a member of a specific work team requires that one be a member of a particular work unit, division, and organization. As we describe below, this fact has potentially important implications for the understanding of the shape of an employee's commitment "profile."

In summary, although the multiple-constituency framework has not been tested extensively, preliminary evidence indicates some value in measuring commitments to more specific foci within the organization. Existing evidence, however, does not negate the value of measuring organizational commitment at a global level. Becker (1992) found fairly strong correlations among global commitment and job satisfaction, turnover intention, and prosocial organizational behavior. Although significant, the increment in prediction contributed by commitment to specific foci was small. It should be kept in mind, however, that when we as researchers measure commitment to the organization as a whole, we are probably measuring employees' commitment to "top management" (Reichers, 1986) or to a combination of top management and more local foci (Becker & Billings, 1993; Hunt & Morgan, 1994). If, on the one hand, our intention is to use commitment as a means of understanding or predicting behavior of relevance to the organization as a whole (or to top management specifically), it would seem that our purpose can be well served with global measures of organizational commitment. If, on the other hand, we are interested in behavior of relevance to more specific constituencies (e.g., the work team), better understanding and prediction might be afforded by a measure of commitment to the relevant constituency.

Integration of the Multidimensional Approaches

As illustrated above, commitment can be considered multidimensional in both its form and focus. These two approaches to developing a multidimensional framework are not incompatible. Indeed, one can envision a two-dimensional matrix with the different forms of commitment listed along one axis and the different foci along the other. The various cells within this matrix then reflect the nature of the commitment an employee has toward each individual constituency of relevance to him or her. Notice that one should not use this matrix to classify employees. Rather, each employee's commitment profile (a multidimensional profile, in this case) would reflect varying degrees of different forms of commitment to each of the different constituencies. An example of what such a matrix would look like is presented in Figure 2.1.

Notice that the top row in Figure 2.1 reflects the commitment model described by Meyer and Allen (1991); that is, employees are viewed as having varying degrees of affective, continuance, and normative commitment to the organization as a whole. The first column in Figure 2.1 reflects Reichers's (1985) multiple constituency approach. In her treatment of commitment, Reichers described commitment primarily as an affective attachment but noted that the attachment can be felt to varying degrees for specific constituencies within (and perhaps beyond) the organization. Thus, this matrix reflects the expansion of Allen and Meyer's model to include multiple constituencies and of Reichers's model to include multiple components of commitment. Potentially, therefore, it should be possible to measure the different forms of commitment to each of the various constituencies and to enter a value into each cell in the matrix to reflect an employee's multidimensional commitment profile.

Considering Meyer and Allen's (1991) and Reichers's (1985) conceptualizations alone, we might conclude that values entered into each cell of the two-dimensional matrix are independent of one another. Lawler's (1992) nested-

‒	*Nature of Commitment*		
Focus of Commitment	*Affective*	*Continuance*	*Normative*
Organization			
Top Management			
Unit			
Unit Manager			
Work Team			
Team Leader			

Figure 2.1. An integration of two multidimensional conceptualizations of commitment

collectives perspective, however, suggests many dependencies among the cells. For example, employees who belong to a local collective (e.g., a work group) must remain with a larger collective (e.g., organization) to continue their membership in the former. Consequently, those who have a strong affective commitment to the local collective (want to belong) might experience a high level of continuance commitment to the larger collective (need to belong). We discuss the nature and potential implications of these dependencies in greater detail in Chapter 6.

Figure 2.1 illustrates that both the conceptualizations provided by Meyer and Allen (1991) and Reichers (1986) are incomplete. Of course, by combining the two we create a complex multidimensional model of commitment that becomes virtually impossible to test or use in its entirety. We are not advocating such a use of this model. Rather, it is presented here to acknowledge the complex multidimensional nature of commitment within the workplace and to raise awareness of the fact that, in trying to understand how employees' commitment develops and relates to behavior, researchers must frame their research questions more precisely than they have in the past. If, for example, we are interested in knowing whether commitment is related to employees' prosocial behavior at work, we must state explicitly in what form of commitment we are interested (Meyer et al., 1993;

O'Reilly & Chatman, 1986). As we discuss in the next chapter, the implications of various *forms* of commitment for on-the-job behavior differ. Similarly, we need to identify clearly what behaviors we are interested in predicting and what *constituency* in the organization is most likely to be affected by this behavior (Becker & Billings, 1993). Behavior that is of direct benefit (or detriment) to a work team might be related more strongly to employees' commitment to the team or team leader than to commitment to the organization as a whole. Nevertheless, researchers should remain aware of the possibility that commitment to other constituencies might also have a complementary or conflicting influence on employees' behavior.

Consequences of
Organizational Commitment

Many claims have been made in the popular press about both the advantages and disadvantages of having a committed workforce. In this chapter, we examine the research evidence linking commitment to various forms of employee behavior. Although the focus of an individual's work commitment may be on any one of several entities (e.g., the work group, the occupation, the organization), our emphasis in this chapter is on commitment to the organization—in particular, whether employees who are strongly committed to their organizations differ from those with weak commitment in terms of turnover, attendance at work, and job performance and whether organizational commitment has implications for employee well-being.

As indicated in Chapter 2, organizational commitment is best thought of as a psychological state linking employees to their organizations. This state is multifaceted in nature. Although other viable classification schemes describe the nature of commitment, the framework used here is that provided by the three-component

23

conceptualization of commitment outlined by Allen and Meyer (1990a; Meyer & Allen, 1991). Thus, in this chapter, we examine the consequences of affective, continuance, and normative commitment to the organization. Drawing on earlier theoretical work (Meyer & Allen, 1991), we begin with a description of and rationale for the hypothesized consequences of these three forms of commitment. This is followed by a review of the research evidence relating to these predictions.

Hypothesized Consequences of Organizational Commitment

It is expected that affective, continuance, and normative commitment will all be related to employee retention; that is, each form of commitment should be negatively correlated with employees' intentions to leave the organization and with voluntary turnover behavior. Meyer and Allen (1991) argued, however, that the three components of commitment have quite different consequences for other work-related behavior, such as attendance, performance of required duties (in-role performance), and willingness to go "above and beyond the call of duty" (extra-role performance or "organizational citizenship" behavior). The basis of this argument, of course, lies in the differences in the psychological nature of each form of commitment.

Given that an employee with strong affective commitment feels emotional attachment to the organization, it follows that he or she will have a greater motivation or desire to contribute meaningfully to the organization than would an employee with weak affective commitment. Thus, it is expected that employees with strong affective commitment will choose to be absent from work less often and will be motivated to perform better on the job.

Such is not the case, however, for employees whose primary link to the organization is based on strong continuance commitment. These employees stay with the organization, not for reasons of emotional attachment, but because of a recognition that the costs associated with doing otherwise are simply too high. All else being equal, there is no reason to expect that such employees will have a particularly strong desire to contribute to the organization. Indeed, it is possible that commitment of this sort, if the sole basis for staying with the organization, could create feelings of resentment or frustration that could lead to inappropriate work behavior. For these reasons, Meyer and Allen (1991) predicted that continuance commitment will be either unrelated or negatively related to attendance and other performance indicators—except in cases where job retention is clearly contingent on performance.

An employee with strong normative commitment is tied to the organization by feelings of obligation and duty. Meyer and Allen (1991) argued that, generally, such feelings will motivate individuals to behave appropriately and do what is right for the organization. Thus, it is expected that normative commitment to the organization will be positively related to such work behaviors as job performance, work attendance, and organizational citizenship. Because feelings of obligation are unlikely to involve the same enthusiasm and involvement associated with affective attachment, however, these relations might be quite modest. In addition, normative commitment might have a particularly important impact on the "tone" with which the work is carried out. For example, employees who remain in an organization primarily because of strong normative commitment might occasionally resent their sense of indebtedness or obligation to the organization. Although this resentment might not prevent them from carrying out particular duties, it could influence how willingly or grudgingly they do so.

Organizational Commitment and Behavior: Research Evidence

We turn now to an examination of the research evidence pertaining to these various propositions. In our review, we describe the pattern of findings and, where relevant, highlight the conditions that appear to influence the strength and direction of the links between commitment and behavior. The reader will notice two defining features of this research. First, the nature of commitment means it is difficult, if not impossible, to manipulate levels of commitment directly. Thus, although we discuss the relations between commitment and work behavior by using cause-and-effect terminology, very few of these "consequence of commitment studies" are designed in a way that fully justifies such language. Second, considerably more attention has focused on affective and continuance commitment than on normative commitment.

Commitment and Employee Retention

As anticipated, the relations between organizational commitment and employee retention variables are well established. Several reviews report consistent negative correlations between organizational commitment and both employee intention to leave the organization and actual turnover (Allen & Meyer, 1996; Mathieu & Zajac, 1990; Tett & Meyer, 1993). Although correlations are strongest for affective commitment, significant relations between commitment and turnover variables are found for all three conceptualizations of commitment (see Allen & Meyer).

On the basis of these findings, it might be tempting to conclude that if an organization's goal is to develop a stable workforce on whose continued membership it can count, any form of commitment will suffice. For the reasons stated above, however, we caution strongly against this conclusion unless employee retention is the organization's *only* goal. An emphasis on employee retention to the exclusion of performance is unlikely to characterize many organizations. Indeed, it is now widely recognized that some voluntary turnover is helpful, rather than harmful, to the organization in that it includes resignations from employees who perform poorly or are disruptive (e.g., Dalton, Krackhardt, & Porter, 1981; Hollenbeck & Williams, 1986). Most organizations—and most managers—want much more from committed employees than simply their continued membership in the organization.

Commitment and Performance at Work

Many aspects of work performance can be assessed (e.g., attendance at work, performance of assigned duties, organizational citizenship behavior). In addition, assessments of performance can be obtained from several sources (e.g., the employees themselves, their supervisors, output measures such as sales or production figures). Research on the links between commitment and work performance reflects this diversity.

Attendance at Work

Several studies have examined the relations between organizational commitment and attendance (or its inverse, absenteeism). As expected, affective commitment is positively related to attendance. In their meta-analysis of data obtained from 23 samples, Mathieu and Zajac (1990) reported a modest mean corrected correlation of .10 between attendance and commitment (most studies used measures of affective commitment). There are several reasons why an employee might be absent from work; theoretically, of course, we would only expect affective commitment to influence attendance in those situations in which the employee had a choice about whether to come to work. That is, although commitment should be negatively correlated with voluntary absence from work, it is not ordinarily expected to be correlated with involuntary absence such as that due to illness or family emergencies. Mathieu and Zajac's meta-analysis included many studies that did not distinguish between voluntary and involuntary absence; thus, we might expect the average correlation that they reported to be somewhat weaker than the correlation between affective commitment and attendance over which employees have personal control (voluntary absence). Four recent studies provide evidence consistent with this possibility.

First, Meyer et al. (1993) asked employees to provide two estimates of absenteeism: (a) total number of days absent and (b) number that were missed because the employee "didn't feel like going to work." The latter was included as a more direct measure of voluntary absence. Although affective commitment was not correlated with the total absence measure (which would include both voluntary and involuntary absence), it did correlate significantly with the measure of voluntary absence ("didn't feel like going").

Second, Hackett, Bycio, and Hausdorf (1994), in a study of bus drivers, found that affective commitment was negatively related to culpable but not nonculpable absences. In other words, employees with strong affective commitment were less likely than those with weak commitment to miss work for reasons that were under their own control. As would be expected, however, affective commitment level was unrelated to absences over which the employee had little control (e.g., illness-related absence).

Third, in a study of hospital employees, Gellatly (1995) collected measures of both total days absent and absence frequency (number of absence incidents regardless of duration) over a 12-month period. Using structural equation modeling analyses, he found that affective commitment contributed to the prediction of absence frequency but not the total-days measure even when several other individual-level and group-level predictors were included in the analysis. This finding is relevant to the present discussion because (a) absence frequency is commonly considered an index of voluntary absence and (b) total days absent is considered indicative of involuntary absence.

Fourth, Somers (1995) reported that although employees with strong affective commitment were no more or less likely to be absent overall, they were significantly less likely to have the more "suspicious" annexed absences (absences connected to a weekend or holiday) on their work attendance records.

In the four studies described above, the correlations between affective commitment and measures that can be considered more voluntary in nature (e.g., annexed absence, culpable absence, absence frequency) are greater than those between affective commitment and involuntary absence and exceed the average correlation reported in the Mathieu and Zajac (1990) meta-analysis. Taken together, the results of these studies suggest that affective commitment is significantly related to voluntary but not involuntary absence and that research in which the two types of absence are combined is likely to underestimate the influence of affective commitment on attendance behavior over which employees have control.

In contrast to affective commitment, absenteeism does not seem to be significantly related to continuance commitment (e.g., Gellatly, 1995; Hackett et al., 1994; Meyer et al., 1993; Somers, 1995). In a recent study of nurses, however, Somers reported that annexed absences were predicted by an interaction between affective and continuance commitment. Specifically, the relation between affective commitment and annexed absence was weaker among nurses with moderate to high levels of continuance commitment than it was among nurses with low levels of continuance commitment. Overall, annexed absences were most common among nurses who had low levels of both affective and continuance commitment. Possibly, annexed absences provided these employees with a temporary means of escape from their organizations—organizations to which they had neither cost-based nor emotional ties.

Finally, the relation between normative commitment and absenteeism has received limited attention. Normative commitment was found to correlate with voluntary absence in one study (Meyer et al., 1993) but not in others (Hackett et al., 1994; Somers, 1995).

In-Role Job Performance

A distinction is made in the literature—and by managers—between those aspects of job performance that represent duties, activities, and accomplishments considered "part of the job" and those that, in essence, go beyond the (implicit or explicit) job description. Although this simplistic distinction is by no means clear-cut, as you will see later, it provides a useful way to categorize job performance. The term *in-role job performance* is used here to refer to the performance of required features of the job.

Relations With Affective Commitment. Results of several recent studies suggest that, overall, employees with strong affective commitment to the organization work harder at their jobs and perform them better than do those with weak commitment. Many of these findings are based on employee reports of their own behavior. Affective commitment has been positively correlated, for example, with various self-reported measures of work effort (e.g., Bycio, Hackett, & Allen, 1995; Ingram, Lee, & Skinner, 1989; Leong, Randall, & Cote, 1994; Randall, Fedor, & Longenecker, 1990; Sager & Johnston, 1989). Affective commitment has also been linked to managers' self-reported adherence to organizational policy. In their study of managers of subsidiary operations within multinational corporations, Kim and Mauborgne (1993) found that those with strong affective commitment to the organization reported higher levels of compliance with strategic decisions made at the corporate level than did those with weaker commitment. Similarly, Nouri (1994) found that managers with strong affective commitment reported that they were more likely to adhere to corporate policy by avoiding "budgetary slack" in their financial planning than were those with low affective commitment. Finally, affective commitment has been positively correlated with self-reported measures of overall job performance in several studies (e.g., Baugh & Roberts, 1994; Darden, Hampton, & Howell, 1989; Johnston & Snizek, 1991; Meyer et al., 1993; Saks, 1995).

The claim that employees with strong affective commitment outperform those with weak commitment does not rely exclusively on studies that use self-reported performance measures, however. Numerous studies have included independent assessments of performance. In some studies, for example, affective commitment has been linked to objective indicators such as sales figures (Bashaw & Grant, 1994) and the control of operational costs (DeCotiis & Summers, 1987). Significant positive relations have also been reported between employees' affective commitment and their supervisors' ratings of their potential for promotion (Meyer et al., 1989) and their overall performance on the job (Konovsky & Cropanzano, 1991; Mayer & Schoorman, 1992; Meyer et al., 1989; Moorman, Niehoff, & Organ, 1993; Sager & Johnston, 1989).

In some studies, affective commitment and performance indicators are not related (e.g., Ganster & Dwyer, 1995; Williams & Anderson, 1991), whereas, in others, commitment is related to one, but not another, performance indicator. Studies of this latter sort, three of which are summarized below, have potential for increasing understanding of the conditions under which significant links between affective commitment and performance will be observed.

DeCotiis and Summers (1987) examined links between commitment and performance indicators within the restaurant business. In this study, restaurant managers were rated by their supervisors on several performance dimensions, none of which correlated with the managers' affective commitment to the organization. Affective commitment was positively related, however, to three objective measures of cost control. Shim and Steers (1994) conducted research in two organizations in the wood products industry. They reported a significant correlation between affective commitment and performance ratings made by supervisors in one of the two organizations but not the other. Finally, Angle and Lawson (1994) examined organizational commitment among employees of Fortune 500 companies within the manufacturing sector. They reported that the affective commitment of employees was unrelated to supervisor ratings of employees' overall performance, organization/accomplishment, and judgment but was significantly correlated with supervisor ratings of employees' dependability and initiative.

These three studies are particularly interesting in that they highlight potential reasons why affective commitment and performance indicators are not significantly related in every study in which they are examined. First, it is possible that any relations between employee commitment and ratings of employee performance made by supervisors (or other subjective raters, such as coworkers) are moderated by the seriousness with which raters take the appraisal process. Consider the study by DeCotiis and Summers (1987) in which supervisor ratings were unrelated to employee commitment. DeCotiis and Summers questioned whether the performance appraisal system was taken at all seriously by the supervisors in their study, noting that although appraisals had been in place for several years, "they had not been used as inputs to personnel decisions such as pay and promotion" (p. 466). If supervisors do not take them seriously, the validity of performance ratings—and therefore the research findings based on these ratings—are in question.

Second, and somewhat related to the above point, is the notion that affectively committed employees direct their attention to aspects of their work performance they believe to be valued by and valuable to the organization. Shim and Steers (1994) conducted follow-up interviews with representatives of the two companies in their study. These interviews revealed that the organization in which commitment was related to performance ratings placed particular emphasis on satisfying customers and on continuous performance improvement. Shim and Steers suggested that this emphasis might have conveyed specific information about what the organization wanted and, in doing so, made clear to employees how they could best express their commitment. Similarly, in interpreting the significant relations they observed between commitment and cost control measures, DeCotiis and Summers (1987) noted that it was on these measures, and not on supervisor ratings, that managers believed their bonuses were based. Taken together, the observations made in these two studies suggest that affective commitment will most likely find expression in those aspects of job performance that employees believe are important to the organization.

Third, the impact of commitment on performance will only be observed to the extent that the performance indicator reflects employee motivation and is relatively unconstrained by other factors (e.g., ability, access to resources). In support of this idea, Angle and Lawson (1994) argued that the variables that correlated significantly with commitment in their study—employee dependability and initiative—represented aspects of performance that are particularly motivational in nature, whereas those that did not correlate significantly with commitment might be more strongly influenced by such nonmotivational factors as employee ability.

Fourth, for affective commitment to influence particular performance outcomes, the employee must have adequate control over the outcomes in question. DeCotiis and Summers (1987) hinted at the importance of this. Recall that they found organizational commitment significantly related to various measures of cost control but not to supervisor ratings. DeCotiis and Summers interviewed senior executives in the company about several issues related to this study and reported that the particular cost-control measures used in the study were ones over which the restaurant managers had considerable personal control. In other words, cost control was one area where the managers could make a difference; those with strong affective commitment were more likely to choose to do so.

Before leaving our discussion of affective commitment and performance indicators, we note that most studies have examined the relations between these variables at the individual level of analysis. This is not surprising, of course, given that organizational commitment is considered an individual-level variable. Nevertheless, a few studies have examined the link between organizational commitment and performance by using a group-level or organization-level analysis.

Mowday, Porter, and Dubin (1974) examined affective commitment among clerical employees in 37 branches of a bank. On the basis of evaluations from the bank's head office, each branch was rated on two branch-level performance indicators: (a) overall customer service and (b) loan performance. Employee commitment (aggregated at the branch level) was related to the customer service measure but not to the loan performance measure. In explaining this finding, Mowday et al. pointed out that the customer service measure reflected activities done by the bank's clerical employees, whereas the loan performance measure reflected activities done mainly by nonclerical staff (e.g., the manager) and done outside the individual branches.

Angle and Perry (1981) correlated the aggregated commitment scores of bus drivers representing 24 bus services with various measures of organizational effectiveness. In this study, commitment was negatively correlated with some outcome measures (e.g., bus service turnover rates, aggregated tardiness) but unrelated to others (e.g., operating expenses of the bus services).

Both these studies used fairly small samples (37 and 24 work units, respectively). A much larger study of organization-level relations between commitment and performance indicators was conducted by Ostroff (1992). In this study, the affective organizational commitment of several thousand junior and senior high school teachers in 298 schools was measured and averaged within each school; that is, a commitment score for each school was calculated, thus treating commitment as an organization-level variable. To justify aggregating commitment scores, Ostroff first demonstrated that consensus (regarding commitment) occurred among teachers within each school and that differences in teacher commitment across schools was meaningful. Ostroff hypothesized and found that (school-level) teacher commitment was correlated with several independent measures of school performance. For example, teacher commitment was correlated positively with average student performance on some academic achievement tests, student attendance, and student satisfaction with their teachers and their education. Commitment was negatively correlated with school dropout rates and a measure of discipline problems within the school. Interestingly, Ostroff also noted that the correlations between commitment and some performance variables tended to be stronger than those reported in studies that used an individual level of analysis.

Various statistical and measurement arguments can be offered to explain this observed difference between levels of analysis (see Ostroff, 1993). It is also possible, however, that individual-level performance indicators, typically used in commitment research, simply do not capture the more unusual expressions of commitment on employee behavior, which when added together significantly improve overall organizational functioning. In addition, affective commitment might prompt employees to consider and modify their contributions at work in the light of skills, preferences, and activities of their coworkers. Although this interdependent approach to work performance is likely to have an important impact on some measures of overall organizational performance, both by reducing redundant behavior and by helping fill gaps, it might not be reflected in traditional individual-level performance indicators.

Overall, the patterns of relations reported in organization-level commitment studies are quite interesting and point to what might be a fruitful direction for future research. Ostroff's (1992) results, in particular, suggest that the approach might be especially appropriate when examining aspects of performance in which the whole is greater than the sum of its parts (e.g., team-based performance, activities in which employees are highly interdependent).

Relations With Continuance Commitment. Like those with strong affective commitment, employees with strong continuance commitment are more likely to stay with the organization than are those with weak commitment (for a summary, see Allen & Meyer, 1996). But that is where the similarity ends. Indeed, available research examining continuance commitment suggests that this particular psychological link to the organization has few positive relations with performance indicators.

Several researchers have reported nonsignificant correlations between continuance commitment and various performance measures (Angle & Lawson, 1994; Bycio et al., 1995; Moorman et al., 1993). Shim and Steers (1994) reported that continuance commitment was unrelated to supervisor ratings in one organization but negatively related in another. Negative correlations have also been observed between continuance commitment and supervisor ratings of potential for promotion (Meyer et al., 1989) and overall job performance (Konovsky & Cropanzano, 1991; Meyer et al.). Finally, Hackett et al. (1994) used a "trained incognito rater" to assess the job performance of bus drivers on a single occasion. Neither this rating nor the number of complaints made against bus drivers was related to continuance commitment. Hackett et al. did find, however, that bus drivers with strong continuance commitment received significantly fewer commendations for their work than did those with weak continuance commitment.

Relations With Normative Commitment. Only a few studies have examined normative commitment and in-role performance indicators. Relations are parallel to, albeit weaker than, those found with affective commitment. Normative commitment has been positively correlated with various self-report measures of work effort (Randall et al., 1990) and with a self-report measure of overall performance (Ashforth & Saks, 1996). Hackett et al. (1994), however, reported no significant relations between normative commitment and independently rated performance indicators.

Citizenship Behavior at Work

For many employees, working involves more than showing up and carrying out required duties. In this section, we turn our attention to research examining the relations between commitment to the organization and those behaviors that many believe are particularly critical to organizational success—the so-called organizational citizenship or extra-role behaviors. The extra-role or organizational citizenship construct has been defined and operationalized in various ways (e.g., Graham,

1991; Katz, 1964; Organ, 1988). Most scholars agree, however, that it includes work-related behavior that "goes above and beyond" that dictated by organizational policy and one's job description. Citizenship, or extra-role, measures typically include such things as providing extra help to coworkers, volunteering for special work activities, being particularly considerate of coworkers and customers, being on time, and making suggestions when problems arise.

As many managers have suspected all along, employees with strong affective commitment appear much more willing to engage in organizational citizenship behavior than those with weak affective commitment. Significant relations between affective commitment and citizenship behavior have been observed in numerous studies involving both self-reports of behavior (Meyer & Allen, 1986; Meyer et al., 1993; Pearce, 1993) and independent assessments of behavior (e.g., Gregersen, 1993; Moorman et al., 1993; Munene, 1995; Shore & Wayne, 1993). In a recent meta-analysis, Organ and Ryan (1995) reported significant average correlations between affective commitment and two forms of organizational citizenship behavior: (a) altruistic acts toward specific members of the organization ($r = .226$) and (b) more generalized compliance with the implicit rules and norms of the organization ($r = .296$).

The relation between normative commitment and citizenship behavior has received much less research attention. In their study of registered nurses, however, Meyer et al. (1993) examined the links between several self-reported measures of citizenship behavior and both affective and normative commitment to the organization. Consistent with earlier predictions (cf. Meyer & Allen, 1991), both affective and normative commitment were positively related to citizenship behavior. The relations between normative commitment and extra-role behavior, however, were weaker than those involving affective commitment.

A quite different pattern emerges when continuance commitment and citizenship behavior are examined. In one study, continuance commitment and citizenship behavior were unrelated (Meyer et al., 1993); in another, they were negatively related (Shore & Wayne, 1993). Moorman et al. (1993) reported weak but significant positive correlations between continuance commitment and some, but not all, of the measures of citizenship behaviors included in their study. Finally, in their meta-analysis, Organ and Ryan (1995) reported that continuance commitment was not related to either altruism or compliance behavior.

Morrison (1994) took a somewhat different approach to the study of extra-role, or citizenship, behavior. She argued that because the boundary between extra-role behavior and in-role behavior is often unclear, the distinction between the two might itself be related to the employees' work attitudes. In her study,

Morrison examined the extent to which behaviors typically considered extra-role would be seen by employees as part of their job. She predicted that both affective and normative commitment would be positively related to how broadly employees defined their jobs; that is, she expected that those with strong affective and normative commitment would see their jobs as encompassing more activities and responsibilities than did those with weak commitment. Results supported both these predictions. In addition, both affective commitment and normative commitment correlated significantly with the (self-reported) tendency to engage in these behaviors. It appears, from these research findings, that the comment "It's not my job" is less likely to be heard from an employee with either strong affective commitment or strong normative commitment than one with weak commitment.

As with in-role behavior (e.g., DeCotiis & Summers, 1987), the organization's message about what is desirable or expected might also moderate links between commitment and extra-role behavior. This point was illustrated in a study by Schaubroeck and Ganster (1991), who examined the willingness of student members in 21 volunteer organizations to engage in an extra-role behavior (telephone fund-raising) on behalf of their organization. Approximately half the students belonged to service organizations and half to nonservice (fellowship or professional) organizations. Schaubroeck and Ganster predicted and found that the relation between members' affective commitment to their organization and their willingness to do the fund-raising was moderated by the purpose of the organization. In service organizations, affective commitment and participation in the fund-raising were positively related; in the nonservice organizations, the two variables were unrelated.

Other Reactions to Work

Commitment has also been found to be related to the way employees respond to dissatisfaction with events at work. Drawing on the work of Hirschman (1970) and Farrell (1983), Meyer et al. (1993) examined three responses to dissatisfaction (in addition to turnover, discussed earlier): voice, loyalty, and neglect. In this study, conducted with a sample of registered nurses, affective commitment was positively correlated with willingness to suggest improvements (voice) and to accept things as they are (loyalty) and negatively correlated with the tendency to withdraw passively from or ignore the dissatisfying situation (neglect). Continuance commitment was unrelated to the likelihood that the nurses would suggest ways to improve the situation or would simply accept the situation. Interestingly, however, the stronger the nurses' continuance commitment, the more likely they were to respond by neglecting or passively withdrawing from the dissatisfying situation.

Employees occasionally face situations in which they believe that the organization has done something unethical or illegal. One response to these situations is whistle-blowing (reporting the organizational practice to people or institutions that might be able to remedy it). It has been suggested that those with strong commitment to the organization would be least likely to engage in whistle-blowing (Randall, 1987); in contrast, others have suggested that strong commitment would make such behavior more likely (Hirschman, 1970). Somers and Casal (1994) examined this question empirically in a study of accountants. Although affective commitment was unrelated to external whistle-blowing, which involves reporting a wrongdoing outside the organization (e.g., to external auditors, the government, news media), Somers and Casal found evidence of a curvilinear (inverted U-shape) relation between affective commitment and internal whistle-blowing. Interestingly, employees with moderate levels of affective commitment reported a greater likelihood that they would divulge a wrongdoing within the organization (e.g., to supervisors, internal auditors) than employees who had either weak or strong affective commitment.

Finally, Wahn (1993) was interested in the relation between continuance commitment and the likelihood that an employee would behave unethically. She argued that because employees with strong continuance commitment are more dependent on the organization than are those with weak continuance commitment, they would be less reluctant to engage in those unethical activities that had relevance for protecting or enhancing their careers. A large sample of human resource professionals employed by several organizations participated in the study. Consistent with her prediction, Wahn reported that continuance commitment was positively correlated with an overall measure of unethical activity. In a more fine-grained analysis, Wahn examined separately the two factors that made up her composite measure of unethical behavior. Although continuance commitment was positively related to compliance with organizational requests to behave in ways deemed "against the interests of the general public to protect your organization" (p. 249), it was not significantly related to self-serving activities done at the expense of others (e.g., blaming a coworker for one's own error). The reason for this difference is not clear. Possibly, employees thought engaging in activities that protected the organization (albeit at the expense of the general public) also provided particularly strong protection for their own jobs, whereas activities done at the expense of individuals did not serve this purpose.

Commitment and Employee Well-Being

Thus far, we have focused on the work-related consequences of organizational commitment. We turn now to the possibility that commitment to the organization has implications for employee well-being and behavior beyond the workplace. Perhaps not surprisingly, the emphasis in the literature is on affective commitment although some research has also examined normative and continuance commitment.

It might be argued that there are personal benefits of strong affective commitment—if for no other reason than it "feels better" to work in an environment about which one feels positively. Some evidence consistent with this argument comes from the stress literature. Several studies have reported significant negative correlations between affective commitment and various self-reported indices of psychological, physical, and work-related stress (Begley & Czajka, 1993; Jamal, 1990; Ostroff & Kozlowski, 1992; Reilly & Orsak, 1991). In one of these studies (Reilly & Orsak), continuance and normative commitment were also examined. Like affective commitment, normative commitment was negatively correlated with several measures of stress-related variables (e.g., work stress, emotional exhaustion, depersonalization); no significant correlations were found, however, between continuance commitment and these measures.

Begley and Czajka (1993) conducted a longitudinal study of hospital employees during a period of organizational restructuring that was described as "very tense" (p. 553). In this study, researchers measured affective commitment and job displeasure (a composite of job dissatisfaction, irritation, and intention to quit) while the organization was operating in its usual mode (before restructuring was even rumored). After restructuring had begun, a second measure of displeasure was taken, and employees were also asked how much stress they experienced as a result of the organizational changes. Interestingly, the stress that employees attributed to the organizational changes was positively correlated with the displeasure they felt, but only for employees with weak affective commitment to the organization. In other words, those with strong affective commitment seemed to be buffered against the impact of stress on displeasure.

It has also been argued that very strong affective commitment to the organization might have deleterious consequences for feelings toward and time spent on important aspects of one's life (e.g., Randall, 1987). Overall, however, the data do not seem to support such a conclusion. Romzek (1989) conducted a longitudinal study of public-sector employees in which she examined the links between affective commitment to the organization and the feelings that employees had about their careers and about various nonwork aspects of their lives. Commitment was positively correlated with both career satisfaction and nonwork satisfaction. Similarly, Kirchmeyer (1992) reported that employees with strong affective commitment to the organization claimed to spend more time on parenting and community activities than did those with weak affective commitment. In a related vein, Cohen and Kirchmeyer (1995) asked employees whether they believed that work interfered with their nonwork experiences. Affective and normative commitment were both unrelated to this belief. Interestingly, however, continuance commitment was positively correlated with the interference belief; that is, employees with strong continuance commitment to the organization were significantly more likely to believe that work interfered with their nonwork experiences.

Clearly, the results of the studies described in this section cannot be considered evidence that either affective or normative commitment to the organization enhances employee well-being. They do seem to refute the claim, however, that affective commitment has negative consequences for life beyond the organization. Moreover, these results suggest the need to examine more closely the link between continuance commitment and employee well-being.

Summary and Conclusions

Taken together, considerable evidence across a wide variety of samples and performance indicators suggests that employees with strong affective commitment to the organization will be more valuable employees than those with weak commitment. Similar, albeit weaker, effects are reported for normative commitment. The picture that emerges from the existing research involving continuance commitment, however, is rather disconcerting. As with affective and normative commitment, employees who believe that strong costs are associated with leaving their organization are unlikely to do so. At the same time, however, they are also less likely to make positive contributions to the organization. Indeed, evidence suggests that employees with strong continuance commitment might be poorer performers, engage in fewer citizenship behaviors, and exhibit more dysfunctional behaviors than those with weak continuance commitment.

Although some have suggested that the magnitude of the relations between affective commitment to the organization and work behavior is disappointingly low (Randall, 1990), our view of the evidence is more positive. In considering the body of research findings, it is important that we keep in mind the following considerations.

First, from a practitioner-oriented view, even small changes in employee performance can have a significant impact on the organization's bottom line (Cascio, 1982) and, as such, can help or hinder the organization's efforts to gain a competitive edge.

Second, as mentioned earlier, any complex behavior (e.g., performance at work) is governed by a variety of factors, including the person's knowledge, skills, and abilities; the resources (e.g., time, equipment, others' expertise) to which he or she has access; and his or her motivation or desire to do the job (Angle & Lawson, 1994). Theoretically, we would expect any work attitude to influence directly only the motivational factors. Given this expectation, even modest commitment-behavior links must be seen as impressive (Johns, 1991).

Third, and related to the latter point, the latitude that employees have to express their attitudes to the organization will vary considerably across performance indicators and across jobs. In some jobs, for example, the timing and performance of required duties are so tightly constrained that employees with strong, medium, and weak commitment will all appear to be performing similarly—because they are. In such situations, the expression of strong affective commitment might only be possible in terms of such variables as organizational citizenship.

Fourth, as pointed out in Chapter 2, the strongest links between affective commitment and behavior will be observed for behavior that is relevant to the constituency to which the commitment is directed. For example, employees with strong attachments to the work group might express this commitment by helping their coworkers but not by carrying out behaviors of direct relevance to the larger organization.

Finally, as Mathieu and Zajac (1990) acknowledged, many links between commitment and employee behaviors might be moderated by other situational factors. For both scientific and practical purposes, we must learn much more about the conditions under which strong affective commitment will be most likely to influence behavior at work and, conversely, those under which the impact of commitment will be reduced. We have already referred to some possible moderating variables (e.g., performance expectations within the organization), and others have been explored in the literature. For example, recent evidence suggests that the relations between affective commitment and performance are moderated by employees' level of financial need (Brett, Cron, & Slocum, 1995) and their career stage (Cohen, 1991).

To this point, it is not exactly clear why continuance commitment should be linked to negative work behaviors. Perhaps some employees with strong continuance commitment believe they are "trapped" in a "no choice" situation; as such, some behaviors might represent concrete ways of exerting control over the situation. Another possibility is that some employees who feel trapped in their organizations react with anger to the situation and, behaving accordingly, produce poorer quality work. It is also possible that strong continuance commitment promotes something similar, psychologically, to learned helplessness (Seligman, 1975); that is, perhaps continuance-committed employees who recognize that they are bound to the organization and believe that they can do little about it respond, not with anger, but in a passive, "going through the motions" manner. Although plausible, none of these suggestions have been examined empirically, leaving us with much to learn about the process through which continuance commitment and behavior are linked.

Finally, we find intriguing the pattern of results from studies examining the well-being of employees. Although it is limited and much more research needs to be done, available data are at least consistent with the idea that affective commitment might have some positive consequences, and continuance commitment some negative consequences, for quality of life beyond the workplace.

Thus far in the book, we have outlined a framework for conceptualizing commitment and have considered the influence of various forms of commitment on several aspects of work and nonwork life. In the next chapter, we examine the development of organizational commitment. This research has important implications for organizational efforts to "manage for commitment," a topic we address in Chapter 5.

Development of
Organizational Commitment

C learly, commitment at work has important consequences for behavior. For this reason, it is important to understand how commitment develops. In this chapter, we summarize the available empirical evidence and describe the antecedents of affective, continuance, and normative commitment and the processes through which they develop. As with earlier chapters, although our focus is on the development of commitment to the organization, it seems likely that the processes outlined here apply to other domains (e.g., occupations, unions) to which employees become committed.

Development of Affective Commitment

Our discussion of the development of affective commitment is divided into three sections. In the first section, we summarize findings from the many studies that have examined potential antecedent variables associated with affective commitment. In the second, we describe the underlying psychological themes that these findings appear to reflect. In the third section, we focus on the mechanisms, or processes, that might be involved in the development of affective commitment.

Antecedents of Affective Commitment

Literally hundreds of studies have examined the correlations between affective commitment and variables hypothesized to be its antecedents. In summarizing this work, we draw on previous reviews (e.g., Mathieu & Zajac, 1990; Mowday et al., 1982), as well as on empirical work conducted since these reviews. Generally, the wide range of variables that have been examined can be categorized as follows: organizational characteristics, person characteristics, and work experiences.

Organizational Characteristics

The literature contains some support for the idea that organizational structure variables influence affective commitment. For example, decentralization has been related to higher affective commitment (Bateman & Strasser, 1984; Morris & Steers, 1980). Overall, however, the evidence regarding these links is neither strong nor consistent (Mathieu & Zajac, 1990). It might simply be that, in forming attitudes toward an organization, employees are more attuned to their own day-to-day work experiences than they are to these less tangible macro-level variables. It is also possible that stronger relations between organizational characteristics and commitment would be observed if they were examined by using an organizational level of analysis.

Recently, attention has been paid in the commitment literature to the ways in which organization-level policies are designed. Many of these studies focus on the extent to which the policies take or are seen to take into account considerations of justice. Justice has been assessed with respect to specific policy issues such as drug testing (Konovsky & Cropanzano, 1991), pay (Schaubroeck, May, & Brown, 1994), and strategic decision making (Kim & Mauborgne, 1993). In all these studies, significant positive correlations were reported between perceptions of the fairness of the policy and affective commitment. We return later to a more detailed discussion of the role of organizational justice in the development of affective commitment.

The manner in which an organizational policy is communicated has also been linked to affective commitment. For example, Konovsky and Cropanzano (1991) reported higher affective commitment among employees who believed that the organization provided them with an adequate explanation for a new drug-testing policy. Greenberg (1994) manipulated the amount of information given and the sensitivity shown in an organizational communication outlining a new policy that banned smoking in the workplace. Both factors had a strong and positive impact on employee acceptance of the organizational policy. (In this study, the employee acceptance measure incorporated a measure of affective commitment.)

Person Characteristics

Research on person characteristics has focused on two types of variables: demographic variables (e.g., gender, age, tenure) and dispositional variables (e.g., personality, values). Overall, relations between demographic variables and affective commitment are neither strong nor consistent. Although some studies have reported gender differences in affective commitment, results of meta-analyses have shown that gender and affective commitment are unrelated (Aven, Parker, & McEvoy, 1993; Mathieu & Zajac, 1990). It is argued that gender differences in commitment, when they are found, are more appropriately attributed to different work characteristics and experiences that happen, in some samples, to be linked to gender (Aven et al.; Marsden, Kalleberg, & Cook, 1993).

Meta-analytic evidence suggests that age and affective commitment are significantly, albeit weakly, related (Mathieu & Zajac, 1990). Moreover, this relation exists even when variables that are often confounded with age (organizational and positional tenure) are controlled (Allen & Meyer, 1993). It is difficult to interpret this relation as unequivocal evidence that growing older influences one's affective commitment, however, because it might be a result of differences among the particular generational cohorts that have been studied. Additionally, older employees might actually have more positive work experiences than do younger employees.

Meta-analytic reviews also report positive relations between organizational tenure and affective commitment (Cohen, 1993a; Mathieu & Zajac, 1990). As with employee age, it is difficult to offer an unequivocal interpretation of the finding. It is possible that employees need to acquire a certain amount of experience with an organization to become strongly attached to it or that long-service employees retrospectively develop affective attachment to their organization ("I have been here 20 years; I must like it"). Alternatively, however, the correlation between tenure and affective commitment might simply reflect the fact that, over time, those who do not develop strong affective attachment to the organization choose to leave it, and thus only the more highly committed employees remain among the longer-tenured group. Finally, recent evidence suggests that when employee age is partialed out of the relation between tenure and affective commitment, correlations are reduced considerably (Allen & Meyer, 1993). Thus, it is possible that the link between organizational tenure and affective commitment to the organization, reported in so many studies, is really because of employee age.

Neither marital status nor educational level appears to be consistently related to affective commitment. As with many of the demographic variables described above, the relations between these variables and commitment might be moderated by other organizational or personal factors.

We turn now to a consideration of dispositional variables. Although some studies have shown that employees with a high need for achievement and a strong work ethic have stronger affective commitment (e.g., Buchanan, 1974), there is scant consistent evidence that individuals with particular personality characteristics are more or less likely to become affectively committed to an organization. If personality variables are involved in the development of affective commitment, it is more likely to be through their interaction with particular work experiences. For example, a person with a strong need for affiliation might develop stronger affective commitment to an organization that emphasizes and encourages teamwork than would a person whose affiliative needs are more modest.

Some evidence does suggest, however, that people's perceptions of their own competence might play an important role in the development of affective commitment. Of the several person characteristics that they examined, Mathieu and Zajac (1990) reported the strongest link between perceived competence and affective commitment. Employees who had strong confidence in their abilities and achievements had higher affective commitment than those who were less confident. At this point, of course, it is difficult to know whether affective commitment to the organization derives directly from true "dispositional self-confidence." Another quite plausible explanation for the observed relation between these two variables, for example, is that competent people were able to choose higher-quality organizations, which in turn inspired stronger affective commitment.

Finally, it has been suggested that there are differences across individuals in the propensity to become committed (Mowday et al., 1982). This suggestion has been tested in two studies. In a 4-year longitudinal study of military newcomers, Lee, Ashford, Walsh, and Mowday (1992) reported that those with high scores on a commitment propensity measure were more likely to report strong affective commitment to the organization and to remain with it than were those with low commitment propensity scores. Similar findings were reported by Pierce and Dunham (1987) in a study of hospital employees. Because the commitment propensity measure used in this research was a composite measure that included personality, expectations, and organizational choice factors, these findings cannot be interpreted as unequivocal evidence of the role of personality in the development of affective commitment. Nonetheless, the possibility suggested by these findings, that individual differences predispose employees to become affectively committed, is intriguing and worthy of further investigation.

Work Experiences

By far, the vast majority of antecedent studies have focused on variables that fall into the very broad category of work experiences. Moreover, with work experience variables, we find the strongest and most consistent correlations with affective commitment across studies. It is important to note that although some of these variables are assessed objectively, much of this research has relied on employees' perceptions of the experiences in question.

The term *job scope* is used to describe several job characteristics that have been linked to employee satisfaction and motivation (Hackman & Oldham, 1980). Several studies have reported strong correlations between these characteristics and affective commitment. Specifically, across many different samples of employees, affective commitment has been positively correlated with job challenge, degree of autonomy, and variety of skills the employee uses (e.g., Colarelli, Dean, & Konstans, 1987; Dunham, Grube, & Castaneda, 1994; Steers, 1977). In their meta-analytic review, Mathieu and Zajac (1990) reported that a composite measure of job scope, incorporating several job characteristic variables, was more strongly correlated with affective commitment than were the individual variables on which the composite measure was based. Subsequent research has corroborated the importance of the job scope variable in predicting affective commitment (e.g., Hackett et al., 1994; Meyer, Bobocel, & Allen, 1991).

Also consistently related to affective commitment are characteristics of the employee's "role" in the organization. Dozens of studies (see Mathieu & Zajac, 1990) have shown that affective commitment is likely to be low among employees who are unsure about what is expected of them (role ambiguity) or who are expected to behave in ways that seem incompatible (role conflict).

Finally, it appears that relations between employees and their supervisors or leaders might also influence the development of affective commitment. In general, affective commitment to the organization is stronger among employees whose leaders allow them to participate in decision making (e.g., Jermier & Berkes, 1979; Rhodes & Steers, 1981) and who treat them with consideration (e.g., Bycio et al., 1995; DeCotiis & Summers, 1987) and fairness (e.g., Allen & Meyer, 1990a). We have touched already on the link between fairness and commitment in the context of specific organizational policy and procedures. Commitment is also related to how fairly organizational policies and other decisions are carried out by supervisors (Gellatly, 1995; Moorman et al., 1993). Moreover, although there are exceptions (e.g., Lowe & Vodanovich, 1995), research generally suggests that affective commitment is more closely related to perceptions of fair treatment than to satisfaction with personal outcomes (Folger & Konovsky, 1989; Sweeney & McFarlin, 1993).

Themes Within the Antecedents Research

Clearly, a wide range of potential antecedent variables, particularly those within the work experience category, are correlated with affective commitment. Although these variables likely represent some common underlying themes, few attempts have been made to discern what these might be; thus, Reichers (1985, p. 467) noted that the "literature is still characterized by a 'laundry list' of significant antecedent or correlate variables."

If one examines the antecedents research closely, however, some common psychological themes do seem to emerge. Specifically, this body of research highlights the importance of work experiences that communicate that the organization is supportive of its employees, treats them fairly, and enhances their sense of personal importance and competence by appearing to value their contributions to the organization. In suggesting these themes, we make no claims that they "capture" all the findings of the antecedents literature or that they represent more than a preliminary framework within which to view this voluminous body of research. Certainly, seen through our particular individual (and cultural) lenses, the themes seem to describe desirable, rather than undesirable, features of working life. This point does not mean, however, that they necessarily represent a set of universal desiderata or that individual or cultural differences in their relations with affective commitment do not exist. In what follows, we elaborate on the themes and organize the relevant research findings around them.

Supportiveness and Fairness. Evidence that organizational supportiveness might play a role in the development of affective commitment comes from several sources. Employee perceptions of support, for example, have been measured directly in several studies using the Survey of Perceived Organizational Support developed by Eisenberger and his colleagues (Eisenberger, Huntington, Hutchison, & Sowa, 1986). Results of these studies suggest strong links between such perceptions and affective commitment to the organization (Eisenberger, Fasolo, & Davis-LaMastro, 1990; Guzzo, Noonan, & Elron, 1994; Shore & Tetrick, 1991; Shore & Wayne, 1993). Research on organizational newcomers report similar findings. New employees who thought the organization treated them in a supportive manner during the first few months of employment expressed particularly strong affective commitment to the organization (e.g., Allen & Meyer, 1990b; Jones, 1986). A particularly vivid example of the influence of organizational supportiveness comes from a study conducted by Sanchez, Korbin, and Viscarra (1995) on the aftermath of Hurricane Andrew in 1992. Victims of the hurricane who received basic tangible support from their employers (e.g., housing, emergency supplies, financial support, meals) exhibited long-term increases in affective commitment.

The role of supportiveness is also illustrated in research that focused on characteristics of the leader and/or supervisor. Affective commitment has been linked to measures of leader consideration (DeCotiis & Summers, 1987; Mathieu & Zajac, 1990), supervisor supportiveness (Mottaz, 1988; Withey, 1988), transformational and transactional leadership (Bycio et al., 1995), and leader-member exchange (Major, Kozlowski, Chao, & Gardner, 1995). Other, albeit less direct, evidence of the importance of supportiveness comes from research reporting stronger affective commitment among employees who believe that their jobs are secure (Ashford, Lee, & Bobko, 1989) and those who see congruence between their own goals and those of the organization (Reichers, 1986; Vancouver, Millsap, & Peters, 1994; Vancouver & Schmitt, 1991).

The antecedents literature also suggests the importance of another theme closely related to supportiveness—that of fairness. One way that organizational fairness is communicated is through the development and enactment of specific policies and procedures that are and are seen to be fair. Considerable evidence supports a link between the procedural justice associated with organizational policies and the affective commitment of employees (e.g., Konovsky & Cropanzano, 1991). Further, research to date (e.g., Folger & Konovsky, 1989; Sweeney & McFarlin, 1993) supports the prediction made by Lind and Tyler (1988) that employees' perceptions about the fairness of the procedures used—rather than satisfaction with their own personal outcomes—might be particularly influential in shaping affective reactions to institutions or authorities. In other words, employees' affective commitment is more strongly influenced by how fairly decisions are made than by whether they always get what they want.

Several studies have reported negative relations between affective commitment and both role ambiguity and role conflict (e.g., Adkins, 1995; Darden et al., 1989; DeCotiis & Summers, 1987; Jamal, 1990; Johnston, Parasuraman, Futrell, & Black, 1990). Although the reasons that role variables relate to affective commitment have not been explicitly examined, it seems quite likely that both supportiveness and fairness are involved. By failing to make expectations clear, for example, the organization increases the frequency with which the employee will make errors, step on toes, fail to meet obligations, and so on. Particularly for new employees, this situation could be seen as quite unfair; the employee is, in essence, being "set up" to experience problems. At the same time, an organization that takes no steps to reduce the potential for these sorts of problems and that allows employees to work with conflicting and ambiguous role expectations is likely to be perceived as quite unsupportive of its employees.

Personal Importance and Competence. Another central theme that emerges from the antecedents literature involves the extent to which employees are made to feel that they make important contributions to the organization. Obviously, there is no single way that organizations convey the importance they place in the contributions of their employees. Employees undoubtedly develop these feelings on the basis of a number of work experiences, some of which also contribute to perceptions of supportiveness and fairness, described above.

For some employees, the importance of their contributions is communicated through the trust the organization appears to place in their work-related judgments. Consistent with this point, affective commitment has been positively related to participation in decision making (Dunham et al., 1994; Rhodes & Steers, 1981), latitude or discretion over activities (DeCotiis & Summers, 1987; Gregersen & Black, 1992), task autonomy (Dunham et al., 1994), receptiveness of management to employee ideas (Allen & Meyer, 1990a; Lee, 1992), and job scope (Marsh & Mannari, 1977; Mathieu & Zajac, 1990; Meyer et al., 1991).

Also relevant here are experiences that directly contribute to employees' perceptions of competence. As indicated earlier, of the various personal characteristics examined in their meta-analyses, Mathieu and Zajac (1990) reported that employees' perceptions of their own competence were most strongly linked to commitment. Although there might be other explanations for this correlation, one possibility is that organizations that provide competence-enhancing experiences, in turn, promote affective commitment. Consistent with this point are numerous reports that affective commitment is related to job challenge (Allen & Meyer, 1990a; Lee, 1992), promotion within the organization (Gaertner & Nollen, 1989; Johnston, Griffeth, Burton, & Carson, 1993), and use of performance-contingent rewards (Williams, Podsakoff, & Huber, 1992).

Thus far, we have summarized the antecedent literature and highlighted some common psychological themes that seem to be reflected in that literature. Unfortunately, this discussion still tells us little about the processes through which an employee's own characteristics, perceptions, and experiences translate into a particular level of affective commitment to the organization. We turn now to a discussion of the mechanisms, or processes, that might be involved.

Behavioral Commitment and the Process of Retrospective Rationality

In Chapter 2, a distinction was made between the behavioral and attitudinal approaches to commitment. We noted that the focus of the behavioral commitment approach is on explaining commitment to a course of action and that the major goal within this research tradition has been to identify the conditions under which an act, once taken, will be likely to continue. Several conditions, or "binding variables," have been suggested, including the irrevocability of the initial act, its publicness, and the volition associated with it (Kiesler, 1971; Salancik, 1977a). Further, and of particular relevance to this discussion, is the proposition that affective commitment to an entity will develop on the basis of behavioral commitment via retrospective rationality or justification processes.

Extending the behavioral commitment perspective to the organizational context, then, suggests the following. Employees will be more likely to remain with an organization if, among other things, they joined the organization of their own volition, they made their choice public, and the decision could not be reversed easily. Then, after taking actions under these conditions and becoming "bound" to continue with the organization, employees will attempt to justify their actions, retrospectively, by developing emotional attachment to the organization.

Considerable support for behavioral commitment predictions has been found in laboratory settings (e.g., Kiesler, 1971). Although a few attempts have been made to study the retrospective rationality process with employees in organizational settings, they are not without methodological shortcomings and have yielded mixed results (Kline & Peters, 1991; Meyer et al., 1991; O'Reilly & Caldwell, 1981). In one of these studies, Meyer et al. assessed binding variables (volition, irrevocability, importance) along with job quality (a composite measure of several desirable work characteristics) and affective commitment to the organization. Of the binding variables, only volition was related to affective commitment. Consistent with a retrospective rationality view of commitment, employees who had greater freedom to accept their job (more volition) expressed significantly stronger affective commitment to the organization they chose than did those with less freedom. Although this evidence is consistent with a retrospective rationality process, it is also possible that the overall quality of the chosen jobs was higher for those who made their choice freely than for those who were more constrained by other factors. When the overall quality of the job was controlled, the relation between volition and affective commitment became nonsignificant. It seems unlikely, therefore, that volition per se influenced commitment ("I chose it, so I must like it"); more important, it appears, was the quality of the job that the person accepted. Although these results cannot be interpreted as evidence that retrospective rationality does *not* occur, neither do they provide much evidence that it does. Moreover, they do provide strong support for an alternate explanation for the development of affective commitment that focuses on the quality of an employee's work experiences.

Finally, it must be acknowledged that retrospective rationality is a very subtle process and, quite likely, occurs very quickly and without the person's awareness. This element makes the process particularly difficult to assess unambiguously in complex settings. For this reason, one should not conclude that retrospective rationality does not influence attitudes; indeed, Staw (1974) provided a very dramatic demonstration that it can happen even in a field setting. To this point, however, the evidence suggests that the role of retrospective rationalization in the development of affective commitment to the organization might be eclipsed by other processes.

Personal Fulfillment

Another process involved in the development of affective commitment is the fulfillment of personal needs. The notion here is very simple: Employees will develop affective commitment to an organization to the extent that it satisfies their needs, meets their expectations, and allows them to achieve their goals. In other words, affective commitment develops on the basis of psychologically rewarding experiences. Despite its apparent simplicity, this explanation of the development of affective commitment raises a number of process-related questions. These include questions about how consciously employees evaluate the quality of their work experiences, the universality of the needs involved, and the role of causal attribution in the development of commitment.

Role of Conscious Awareness

It is possible that the emotional attachment an employee develops to the organization comes about simply and quite "unconsciously" through the repeated association of psychologically fulfilling experiences with the organization. This process—which is essentially classical conditioning—would only require that temporal and/or physical proximity exist between the organization and the positive experiences but not that employees be consciously aware of the value of what they are experiencing or why they are experiencing it. For supportiveness to influence affective commitment, for example, it would not be necessary for employees to recognize explicitly that they were in a supportive environment or that the source of the support was the organization. The positive effect resulting from supportive experiences simply becomes associated with or transfers to other "stimuli" in the employees' environment, including the organization. The psychological literature contains ample evidence that classical conditioning influences affective reactions to a wide variety of stimuli (Byrne & Clore, 1970; Gleitman, 1981). Thus, although direct evidence would be difficult to collect in complex organizational settings, there is no apparent reason why this rather basic psychological process would not apply to the development of work-related affect.

This point does not mean, of course, that employees do not engage in quite conscious evaluation of their workplace experiences or that these evaluations do not influence their affective commitment. Indeed, we suspect that most employees reflect quite frequently and explicitly on the pros and cons associated with various aspects of their working life. Experiences that employees find particularly satisfying are likely to increase the affective commitment felt toward the organization; those experiences that are not satisfying will either have no impact on commitment or lessen it.

Individual Difference and Universal Approaches

The premise that a universal set of experiences exists that employees find rewarding and to which they will respond similarly is implicit in the antecedents literature. Indeed, this body of research suggests some themes, outlined earlier in the chapter, that might describe what people generally need in order to become affectively committed to the organization. The universal approach, however, does not explain all the variance in affective commitment. Given that individuals differ in various ways (e.g., personality, values, needs, expectations), it seems likely that these differences will have implications for which workplace experiences employees would find particularly rewarding or fulfilling.

According to this individual-difference approach, personal characteristics will moderate the strength of the relation between a particular work experience and affective commitment (cf. Mathieu & Zajac, 1990). Research has examined this possibility from two perspectives: one that focuses on the expectations that employees have and the other that focuses on personal values.

Met Expectations. Inevitably, employees enter an organization with a set of expectations about what they will encounter. It is possible that these expectations moderate the extent to which a particular experience will be related to affective commitment (Wanous, 1992). The idea here is that positive work attitudes develop when a newcomer's expectations about the job and/or organization are confirmed by his or her experiences. Negative work attitudes develop, however, if those expectations are disconfirmed. Interestingly, this finding suggests that it is not experiences per se that influence affective commitment, but rather the discrepancy (or lack thereof) between those experiences and what the person expects. Extensions of this reasoning suggest that, through their recruitment, selection, and early socialization strategies, employers would be wise to encourage low, rather than high, expectations among organizational newcomers because low expectations can be more easily met (Wanous, Poland, Premack, & Davis, 1992).

Although the notion of met expectations has been incorporated into many streams of organizational research, the empirical relation between met expectations and commitment has only recently been reviewed meta-analytically (Wanous et al., 1992). In this research, Wanous et al. reported an average correlation of .39 between the extent to which employees' expectations were met and their affective commitment to the organization. On this basis, one could conclude that the extent to which a person's expectations are met is important in the development of affective commitment.

More recent evidence provided by Irving and Meyer (1994), however, calls into question this particular process. Drawing from person-job fit research (Edwards, 1991, 1993, 1994; Edwards & Cooper, 1990), Irving and Meyer pointed out a number of methodological shortcomings that characterize the met-expectations studies included in Wanous et al.'s (1992) meta-analysis. These shortcomings include use of difference scores between expectations and experiences, measures of expectations and experiences that are not commensurate, and measures of met expectations that are obtained retrospectively from subjects rather than by comparing actual expectations and experiences. Irving and Meyer conducted a study of newcomers that addressed these methodological problems and found scant support for the met expectations hypothesis. Their results suggest that the quality of employees' work experiences plays a much greater role in the development of affective commitment than does the extent to which preentry expectations are met.

Person-Job Fit. People also differ in terms of their needs, values, and personalities. Research within the person-job fit tradition argues that an experience that is congruent with one person's values or that meets his or her needs will be rewarding to the person and thus will influence affective commitment. But because it may have no relevance for another person, that same experience would not be expected to have an impact on his or her affective commitment.

Only a few tests of this individual-difference perspective have been conducted (Blau, 1987; Meglino, Ravlin, & Adkins, 1989; Meyer, Irving, & Allen, in press; O'Reilly et al., 1991; Vancouver & Schmitt, 1991). Moreover, these studies have provided mixed and sometimes equivocal results. For example, the results of those studies that used difference scores (Meglino et al.; Vancouver & Schmitt) or profile similarity indices (O'Reilly et al.) as measures of person-job fit are difficult to interpret for the reasons outlined by Edwards and his colleagues (Edwards, 1991, 1993, 1994; Edwards & Cooper, 1990). Even when these fit measures correlate with commitment, one cannot rule out the possibility that the correlations reflect the influence of either or both of the person and situation variables alone.

Studies that have tested for the moderating effect of individual differences on the relations between situational characteristics and commitment (Blau, 1987; Meyer et al., in press), rather than for the effect of person-job fit per se, have yielded mixed results. Blau found no evidence for a Person × Situation interaction, whereas Meyer et al. did. The findings reported by Meyer et al., however, were not entirely consistent with expectation. For example, they found that experiences that added to employees' comfort in the organization had their strongest impact on employees who valued such experiences but that the opposite was true for competence-related experiences; that is, the impact of competence-bolstering experiences on affective commitment was greater for those who placed *less* emphasis on such experiences. Although this unexpected result was found in two samples in the Meyer et al. study, only speculative explanations for it could be offered.

It is important to note that the research examining the individual-difference approach to the development of affective commitment is at a relatively early stage. At this point, evidence suggests that the extent to which employees' experiences meet their expectations has relatively little impact on affective commitment. More promising is the suggestion that other individual differences (e.g., values) moderate the effect of work experiences. From the research described here, it appears that some person characteristics and work experiences do have a joint impact on affective commitment. Clearly, however, much more research is needed to clarify the nature and form of that impact.

Universally Rewarding Work Experiences. In considering individual differences, we do not rule out the possibility of some very general characteristics of work that most people will find rewarding and that will enhance their affective commitment to the organization. Earlier in the chapter, we identified some basic themes that emerged from the antecedent research but made no claims about their universal nature. It is interesting to note, however, that these themes— supportiveness, justice, and importance/competence—are echoed in other theorizing about the psychological attachments that people form. As an example, it is now recognized that concerns about procedural justice are quite basic and do much to shape interpersonal contexts (e.g., Tyler & Bies, 1990). Indeed, in their group value model of procedural justice, Lind and Tyler (1988) argued that commitment to social groups (e.g., a work organization) can only be sustained if the person believes that, in the long run, desired outcomes will be distributed fairly. Another of our themes, that involving competence, has been highlighted by researchers working in the area of intrinsic motivation (e.g., Deci & Ryan, 1991). In particular, it has been argued that the development and maintenance of intrinsic motivation for an activity depends, in part, on the competence-enhancing experiences associated with the activity.

Although the themes we derived from the antecedents research might have some merit, we readily acknowledge that there might be much better and more parsimonious ways to summarize this body of research and to identify work experiences that have universal appeal. One possibility, for example, is a much "higher-order" need for experiences that enhance a person's sense of self-worth. Thus, experiences that provide support, involve fair treatment, and communicate that one's contributions are valuable might all increase affective commitment by fulfilling this more basic need to feel good about oneself. At this point, of course, this is only speculative. It is worth noting, however, that notions of self-worth or self-esteem are central to several psychological theories (e.g., social identity theory; Tajfel, 1982).

Role of Causal Attribution

Experiences that employees find fulfilling have many sources within the workplace (e.g., coworkers, the job, the organization). Moreover, an organization can provide a particular positive experience for a variety of reasons (e.g., compliance with the law, out of habit, genuine concern for employees). This point raises a question about the role of causal attributions. Do employees' evaluations of either the motivation for or source of a fulfilling work experience influence the extent to which that experience will increase affective commitment?

Recent developments in the commitment literature suggest that causal attributions might very well play an important role in the development of affective commitment. Koys (1988, 1991) reported that the impact of desirable human resource management practices on commitment was moderated by employees' perceptions of the motives for these practices. To the extent that employees believed that the practices were motivated by concern and respect for employees, they reported stronger affective commitment. When employees believed that the practices were implemented to comply with legislative changes, however, the practices were unrelated to affective commitment.

Meyer and Allen (1995) were interested in the extent to which commitment was influenced by the attributions that employees made about the source of positive work experiences. They examined relations between work experiences and affective attachment to three domains: the job, the supervisor, and the organization. Meyer and Allen hypothesized and found that relations between work experiences and affective reactions to each domain were moderated by the extent to which employees attributed them to the domain in question.

Results of these studies are interesting for three reasons. First, they provide evidence that attributional processes are involved in the development of affective commitment to the organization. Second, in doing so, they suggest that conscious awareness must play some role in the process; presumably, if classical conditioning alone were involved, the attributions that employees made for their positive work experiences would have no influence on their commitment. Third, these results might help in explaining the variability, found across studies, in the strength of the links between particular work experiences and affective commitment to the organization. In those studies in which weaker relations were found, employees might have had reason to attribute the work experience to another domain (e.g., the supervisor, the occupation) or to make the assumption that the organization provided the experience for reasons other than concern for its employees.

Summary

Considerable research attention has been focused on the development of affective commitment. This research has identified a wide array of potential antecedent variables and suggested several process variables that might be involved. We see the processes proposed here as complementary, rather than as competing.

Although the evidence for it is limited, retrospective rationality might well be operative in some situations. Affective commitment also develops on the basis of work experiences that employees find rewarding or fulfilling. Some evidence suggests that the fulfillment of individual (as opposed to universal) needs is important in the development of affective commitment. These results are far from consistent, however, and much more research is needed to clarify the manner in which individual characteristics and work experiences interact. On the basis of the antecedents research, we suggested possible universal appeal for those work environments in which employees are supported, treated fairly, and made to feel that they make important contributions. Further, such experiences might fulfill a higher-order desire to enhance perceptions of self-worth. A refinement of these themes awaits further investigation. Finally, it appears that the impact of work experiences on affective commitment to the organization might be greater to the extent that employees attribute the experience to the organization and believe it to be motivated by a concern for employees.

Development of Continuance Commitment

Recall that *continuance commitment* refers to the employee's awareness that costs are associated with leaving the organization. Employees who have strong continuance commitment to an organization stay with the organization because they believe they *have to* do so. Conceptually, the development of continuance commitment is fairly straightforward. Continuance commitment can develop as a result of any action or event that increases the costs of leaving the organization, provided the employee recognizes that these costs have been incurred. In their three-component model of organizational commitment, Meyer and Allen (1991) summarized these actions and events in terms of two sets of antecedent variables: investments and alternatives. Our discussion of the development of continuance commitment is organized somewhat differently from the discussion of affective commitment. We begin by clarifying what is meant by investments and alternatives and outline the process considerations associated with the development of continuance commitment. This is followed by a description and summary of the relevant empirical evidence.

Investments, Alternatives, and Process Considerations

The notion of investments draws, in part, on Becker's (1960) theorizing about commitment. Becker argued that commitment to a course of action results from the accumulation of side bets a person makes. *Side bets* are actions that link a person to a particular course of action by virtue of the fact that something would be forfeited if he or she discontinued the activity. For example, betting a friend that you will get an A in a course "commits" you to work hard to make it happen. In an application of this notion to organizational commitment, then, a side bet involves the investment of something valuable (e.g., time, effort, money) that an employee would lose if he or she left the organization. Employees can make investments in organizations in many ways, including, for example, by incurring the expense and human cost of relocating a family from another city or by spending time acquiring organization-specific skills. Leaving the organization could mean that the employee would stand to lose or have wasted the time, money, or effort that was invested.

The other hypothesized antecedent of continuance commitment is the employee's perceptions of employment alternatives. Employees who think they have several viable alternatives will have weaker continuance commitment than those who think their alternatives are few. In other words, the perceived availability of alternatives will be negatively correlated with continuance commitment. As with investments, several events or actions can influence one's perceptions of alternatives. For example, one employee might base his or her perception on the external environment, taking a cue from employment rates and the general economic climate. Another employee might base perceived alternatives on the degree to which his or her skills seem current and marketable (vs. outdated and unmarketable). Perceptions of alternatives can also be influenced by such things as the results of previous job search attempts, whether other organizations have tried to recruit the employee, and the extent to which family factors limit the employee's ability to relocate.

With respect to process considerations, it is important to reiterate that neither investments nor alternatives will have an impact on continuance commitment unless or until the employee is aware of them and their implications. Thus, an employee's *recognition* that investments and/or lack of alternatives has made leaving more costly represents the process through which these investments and alternatives influence continuance commitment. (This recognition also differentiates continuance commitment from behavioral commitment; see Chapter 2.)

The fact that recognition plays a central role in this process raises two additional points. First, it means that people who are in objectively similar situations can have quite different levels of continuance commitment. Consider, for example, two employees who have invested considerably in the acquisition of organization-specific skills (e.g., mastery of the company's customized information system) at the expense of more transferable skills (e.g., mastery of generic computer skills). Employee A recognizes that such actions tie him or her to the organization, whereas Employee B does not. This particular investment, therefore, will increase the continuance commitment to the organization felt by Employee A but have no immediate influence on that of Employee B. It is important to note, however, that because Employee B actually did make the investment, it has the potential to influence his or her continuance commitment at some point in the future. Second, for some cost-related variables to influence continuance commitment, a particular "triggering" event might be required—that is, one that focuses the employee's attention on those variables. For example, Employee B might come quickly to realize that his or her skills are not transferable on hearing about the unsuccessful job search of a similarly trained coworker. At this point, his or her investments will have an impact on continuance commitment.

Finally, we note that the specific set of variables that influence an employee's continuance commitment might be quite idiosyncratic to that person. Further, it can include both work-related (e.g., pension contributions) and nonwork-related (e.g., family unable to relocate) variables. Despite this complexity, empirical research examining the development of continuance commitment generally supports the notions outlined above.

Empirical Evidence

Investments and Alternatives

Continuance commitment has been shown to be related to employees' perceptions about the transferability of their skills (Allen & Meyer, 1990a; Lee, 1992;

Withey, 1988) and their education (Lee, 1992) to other organizations. In these studies, employees who thought their educational or training investments were less easily transferable elsewhere expressed stronger continuance commitment to their current organization.

Whitener and Walz (1993) developed a composite measure of side bets that included other sorts of investments that employees might forfeit by leaving their organizations (e.g., retirement money, status, job security). As expected, this measure was positively correlated with continuance commitment to the organization.

Jayne (1994) examined organizational commitment among a sample of employed parents of young children. She reported that employees who strongly identified with the "provider role" (e.g., the only or primary wage earner) had stronger continuance commitment than those who weakly identified with this role. This finding is consistent with what has been hypothesized about the development of continuance commitment. Presumably, employees who take their role as providers more seriously are more aware of the costs associated with leaving the organization.

Employees' perceptions of employment opportunities that are available to them have been correlated with continuance commitment in several studies (Allen & Meyer, 1990a; Lee, 1992; Meyer et al., 1991). Although the measures of perceived alternatives differ, all are negatively correlated with continuance commitment, as would be expected. In addition, continuance commitment is related negatively to employees' perceptions about the attractiveness of alternatives (Whitener & Walz, 1993). This finding suggests that employees evaluate alternatives not only in terms of their availability but also in terms of their viability for them personally.

In their study of bank tellers, Whitener and Walz (1993) also used unemployment rates as a more objective measure of availability of alternatives. They assigned to each bank teller the unemployment rate within his or her geographical region. Interestingly, this measure was not correlated with continuance commitment. It might be that people simply do not see the prevailing unemployment rate as having personal relevance, an inference supported within Whitener and Walz's own data by the fact that the unemployment rate and the attractiveness of alternatives were uncorrelated. Considered in this light, the fact that employment availability (unemployment rate) and continuance commitment are unrelated is consistent with the idea that individual *recognition* of cost-related factors is necessary for those factors to have an impact on continuance commitment.

Employee Age and Organizational Tenure

Many potential antecedents of continuance commitment are of the sort that can accumulate over time. For this reason, some researchers have used time-based variables (e.g., age, tenure) as antecedent measures of continuance commitment (e.g., Alutto, Hrebiniak, & Alonso, 1973; Ferris & Aranya, 1983; Ritzer & Trice, 1969). Findings obtained in these studies have been mixed and should be interpreted with some caution. For some employees, the perceived costs associated with leaving an organization will increase as they get older and increase their organizational tenure. For other employees, however, the costs of leaving might actually decrease; as experience and skills increase, an employee's value to other employers might increase. For this reason, age and tenure are best thought of as proxy or surrogate variables of accumulated investments and perceived alternatives and not as direct predictors of continuance commitment (cf. Cohen & Lowenberg, 1990; Meyer & Allen, 1984).

Summary

The development of continuance commitment has received less research attention than the development of affective commitment. This is, in part, because adequate measures of continuance commitment are a fairly recent addition to the commitment literature (cf. Cohen & Lowenberg, 1990; Meyer & Allen, 1984). Available research evidence is consistent, however, with the idea that continuance commitment to an organization develops as a function of various investments that an employee makes and the employment alternatives that he or she believes exist. Further, some evidence (Whitener & Walz, 1993) is consistent with the view that continuance commitment develops on the basis of employee awareness; for investments or alternatives to influence continuance commitment, the person must be aware of their implications.

Development of Normative Commitment

Normative commitment refers to an employee's feelings of obligation to remain with the organization. Thus, employees with strong normative commitment will remain with an organization by virtue of their belief that it is the "right and moral" thing to do (Meyer & Allen, 1991; Scholl, 1981; Wiener, 1982). Our discussion of normative commitment begins with an outline of earlier (Meyer &

Allen; Wiener) and more recent (Rousseau, 1995) theorizing of relevance to the development of normative commitment. This is followed by a description of the empirical evidence and a discussion of implications for future research.

Hypothesized Antecedents and Processes

Wiener (1982) argued that normative commitment to the organization develops on the basis of a collection of pressures that individuals feel during their early socialization (from family and culture) and during their socialization as newcomers to the organization. Socialization experiences, whether in early life or from one's employer, are extremely rich and varied and carry with them all sorts of messages about the appropriateness of particular attitudes and behaviors. The presumed process here is one of internalization. Through complex processes involving both conditioning (rewards and punishments) and modeling (observation and imitation of others), individuals learn what is valued and what is expected of them by the family, the culture, or the organization. In the case of normative commitment, what gets internalized is a belief about the appropriateness of being loyal to one's organization. By necessity, familial and cultural socialization focuses on the appropriateness of organizational loyalty in quite general terms ("People should not job hop"). Organizational socialization, of course, focuses on the particular organization to which the employee belongs.

It has also been suggested that normative commitment develops on the basis of a particular kind of investment that the organization makes in the employee—specifically, investments that seem difficult for employees to reciprocate (Meyer & Allen, 1991; Scholl, 1981). These might include such things as organization-sponsored tuition payments made on behalf of employees or a "nepotism" hiring policy that favors employees' family members. Given norms of reciprocity (Gouldner, 1960), it is argued that employees might find this sort of imbalance or indebtedness uncomfortable and, to rectify the imbalance, will feel a sense of obligation (normative commitment) to the organization. It is possible that individual (and cultural) differences exist in the extent to which people have internalized reciprocity norms and, therefore, in the extent to which organizational investments will lead to feelings of indebtedness.

Finally, and closely related to the above, normative commitment might also develop on the basis of the "psychological contract" between an employee and the organization (Argyris, 1960; Rousseau, 1989, 1995; Schein, 1980). *Psychological contracts* consist of the beliefs of the parties involved in an exchange relationship regarding their reciprocal obligations. Unlike more formal contracts, psychological contracts are subjective and, therefore, might be viewed somewhat differently by the two parties. Psychological contracts are also subject to change over time as one or both parties perceive obligations to have been fulfilled or violated (Robinson, Kraatz, & Rousseau, 1994). Thus, for example, it might be that an employee who initially responds to an organizational investment with feelings of indebtedness will later reevaluate these feelings if it is determined that the organization has violated some other aspect of the psychological contract. Finally, psychological contracts can take different forms, the most widely recognized of which are *transactional* and *relational* (MacNeil, 1985; Rousseau, 1989). Transactional contracts tend to be somewhat more objective and based on principles of economic exchange, whereas relational contracts are more abstract and based on principles of social exchange. Of the two forms, relational contracts seem more relevant to normative commitment; in contrast, transactional contracts might be involved in the development of continuance commitment (Rousseau & Wade-Benzoni, 1995).

Theory and research on the psychological contract have focused on its links to affective commitment and, to a lesser extent, continuance commitment (see Rousseau & Wade-Benzoni, 1995). The literature contains suggestions, however, that the specific form of commitment most closely associated with psychological contracts differs somewhat from both of these. For example, Robinson et al. (1994) observed that commitment characterized by affective attachment or identification (affective commitment) or by investments in the organization (continuance commitment) "touch on but do not directly confront the role of obligations, reciprocity, and fulfillment" (p. 149). Normative commitment, with its distinct emphasis on obligations, might well be the "missing link" in our understanding of the influence of psychological contracts on employee commitment.

Relevant Empirical Evidence

Of the three forms of commitment described in the three-component model, least is known empirically about the development of normative commitment. Some, albeit limited, evidence relevant to the role played by early socialization comes from a study by Meyer et al. (1993). These researchers developed a measure reflecting a very generalized belief in and need to fulfill one's obligations to others—a view that likely would be shaped by one's early socialization. Interestingly, this measure was not correlated with affective commitment to either the organization or the occupation; it was significantly correlated, however, with normative commitment and continuance commitment to both these domains.

Unfortunately, despite calls for research examining the impact of "early socialization and role modeling" on normative commitment (Dunham et al., 1994, p. 379), to our knowledge no research examines directly the impact of parental values or behaviors on normative commitment to the organization.

Some evidence regarding cultural values comes from a study by Vardi, Wiener, and Popper (1989). They compared two organizations that were similar in all but one respect: the extent to which their organizational values (or mission) were congruent with the core values of the society in which they operated. Vardi et al. predicted and found that employees in the organization whose mission was consistent with cultural values had stronger normative commitment to the organization than did those in the other organization. In this study, normative commitment was compared across organizations within the same culture. Another analytic approach to cultural socialization, of course, would involve explicit cross-cultural comparisons. For example, one might expect that cultures that emphasize collectivist values and lengthy employer-employee relations might experience higher aggregate levels of normative commitment than do cultures characterized by individualist values and greater employment mobility. Although this argument is not new to the commitment literature (e.g., Lincoln, 1989), it has been made with respect to affective commitment. To the extent that the cultural variation described here reflects teachings about what one "ought" to do, however, we would expect to see it expressed in normative commitment, rather than in affective commitment.

Some evidence consistent with the idea that socialization within the organization might influence normative commitment was provided in research conducted by Dunham et al. (1994). Arguing that coworkers send each other signals about what is expected, they predicted and found in two samples significant correlations between employees' normative commitment and that of their coworkers.

On the basis of several studies, it appears that many of the work experiences that predict affective commitment—particularly those associated with supportiveness—are also related, albeit less strongly, to normative commitment (for a summary, see Allen & Meyer, 1996). In a study of newly hired business school graduates, Ashforth and Saks (1996) reported that normative commitment was related to organizational socialization tactics that provided employees with a more institutionalized (rather than individualized) set of early experiences. These findings parallel earlier work in which the tactics were used to predict affective commitment (Allen & Meyer, 1990b; Jones, 1986). Although the reason for these parallel sets of findings is not immediately clear, it might simply be that some types of positive experiences influence feelings of emotional attachment and feelings of obligation at the same time.

Summary

Thus far some, albeit quite limited, evidence suggests that normative commitment develops on the basis of early socialization processes. For the most part, work on the development of normative commitment has been theoretical rather than empirical. We look forward to further work examining the influence of socialization experiences and other processes on the development of normative commitment. Although we still have much to learn about the nature and development of psychological contracts, they appear to hold considerable promise in enhancing our understanding of employment relationships, both generally (Shore & Tetrick, 1994) and with respect to the development of normative commitment. Moreover, acknowledging the existence of normative commitment as relatively distinct from affective and continuance commitment might help in clarifying some of the present confusion regarding the impact on commitment of the fulfillment or violation of the psychological contract.

Summary and Conclusions

In this chapter, we outlined theory and research relevant to the development of the three components of commitment. Although our knowledge contains gaps, research findings are generally consistent with theoretical predictions (Meyer & Allen, 1991).

We have suggested personal fulfillment as the main process through which affective commitment develops. Taken together, the research suggests that employees find particularly fulfilling work experiences that signify supportiveness, justice, and the importance the organization places on employees' contributions. In suggesting a personal fulfillment (or need satisfaction) process, we note that it raises questions about how consciously employees evaluate their work experiences and whether the relevant needs are individual or universal in nature. More work is needed to address these and other process-related issues (e.g., causal attribution).

Existing research suggests that strong continuance commitment develops on the basis of investments and (a lack of) alternatives that influence the costs associated with leaving the organization. This point is consistent with theoretical prediction (e.g., Farrell & Rusbult, 1981; Meyer & Allen, 1991). The critical process variable, and one that requires further empirical investigation, is the employee's recognition that these costs would be incurred and that they are what "tie" him or her to the organization.

Finally, some evidence, consistent with theory, suggests that normative commitment to the organization develops on the basis of pre- and postentry socialization experiences. Of the three components, however, the gap between theory and empirical evidence is widest in the case of normative commitment.

In considering the research on the development of commitment, three additional points should be noted. First, although the processes believed to be involved in the development of these components have been described separately, they occur, to a large extent, in concert. As such, what is described in this chapter represents a somewhat simplified description of the complex relationship between the employee and the organization. Second, our primary focus here has been on theoretical constructs and processes involved in the development of commitment and less on operational factors. In the following chapter, we examine how more specific organizational policies and practices play a role in these processes, with a particular focus on affective commitment. Third, the spotlight in this chapter has been on commitment to the organization. Although this focus represents the domain in which most theoretical and empirical commitment research has been conducted, it is clear that people develop commitment to various work-related domains (e.g., work groups, unions, occupations). In Chapter 6, we discuss commitment to some of these other important domains and consider issues of compatibility and conflict among multiple commitments.

5

Managing for Commitment

As we noted in Chapter 4, *perceptions* play an important role in the development of employees' commitment to the organization. For example, employees who believe that their organizations are supportive tend to become affectively committed. Those who recognize that they have made substantial investments that would be lost if they were to leave the company develop continuance commitment. Those who think that "loyalty" is expected of them become normatively committed. It follows then, that to "manage" commitment, organizations must influence employees' perceptions.

The amount of empirical research conducted to examine the impact of management practices on commitment is limited. We focus our attention here on two areas of management research where commitment has been examined as an outcome variable: human resource management (HRM) and the management of change. The former involves the day-to-day management of people and is therefore an obvious, albeit somewhat recent, topic of research. Interest in the latter stems from the fact that, as we noted in Chapter 1, organizations are undergoing tremendous pressure to change the way they do business to remain competitive. These changes often involve the elimination and reorganization of jobs that affect employees in various ways, including their commitment.

To begin, we provide a theoretical framework to serve as a basis for subsequent discussion. This is followed by a summary of research examining the links between management practices and commitment. Because the research to date is limited, we caution against using any particular finding as the basis for the design of management policy or practice. Nevertheless, recognizing the importance of basing policy and practice on empirical evidence, we conclude this chapter with a discussion of how the findings reviewed here, in conjunction with those presented in Chapter 4, can be used to guide the development of policy and practice. We also identify limitations in existing research to serve as an impetus for additional research in this important area.

A Theoretical Framework

To date, most of the discussion and research concerning the influence of management practices on employees' commitment has focused on affective commitment. There are two good reasons for this focus. First, only recently have multidimensional models of commitment and appropriate measures been developed (see Chapter 2). Second, affective commitment is arguably the most desirable form of commitment and the one that organizations are most likely to want to instill in their employees (see Chapter 3). Nevertheless, it is important to recognize that organizations, through their management practices, can influence employees' continuance and normative commitment as well. In some cases, the same practices can produce different forms of commitment, depending on how they are perceived. Consequently, efforts to foster one form of commitment can inadvertently lead to the development of another. In Figure 5.1, we illustrate how a particular HRM practice can, by activating different mechanisms, influence all three components of organizational commitment.

Figure 5.1 includes only some of the mediating mechanisms identified in Chapter 4. Nevertheless, with this framework in mind, consider how a specific organizational HRM practice, such as training, might lead to different forms of commitment. Employees who receive training, particularly training intended to provide them with the opportunity for advancement, might perceive that the organization values them as individuals (which bolsters their sense of self-worth) and therefore develop a stronger affective commitment. This same training opportunity could lead to the development of continuance commitment, however, if it is perceived as providing organization-specific skills that contribute to status or economic advantage within the company but that will not transfer to jobs outside the organization. Finally, employees who are aware of the expense of training or appreciate the skills they have acquired might develop a sense of obligation (normative commitment) that will hold them in the organization at least long enough to allow them to reciprocate. Similar scenarios can be envisioned for other management practices (e.g., compensation, promotion, downsizing).

Because of the nature of the literature, our review necessarily emphasizes the implications of management practices for the development of affective commitment. Where appropriate, however, we draw attention to how particular practices could also affect other forms of commitment. It must also be recognized, of course, that organizations have many objectives other than developing commitment. We do not mean to imply that commitment is the only or even the most important objective that organizations should have for any particular action they take. What we do want to draw attention to is the fact that management practices, whether designed to or not, can affect commitment.

Human Resource Management Practices

As we noted, only recently have the links between HRM practices and employee commitment been examined empirically. Ogilvie (1986) and Gaertner and Nollen (1989) were among the first to investigate whether employees' perceptions of their organizations' HRM practices were related to affective commitment. Ogilvie conducted interviews with managers from an agriculture production company to determine their assessments of level of pay, accuracy of the merit rating system, fairness of promotions, and comparability of fringe benefits. Three of the four ratings (level of pay, accuracy of merit rating, and fairness of promotion) were found to correlate significantly with commitment. Moreover, perceptions of the accuracy of merit ratings and fairness of promotion were found to contribute over and above personal and work characteristics (e.g., experience, supervision) in explaining differences in commitment level. Gaertner and Nollen found that perceptions of the organization's adherence to career-oriented employment practices, including internal promotion, training and development, and employment security, were related to commitment among employees in a Fortune 100 manufacturing firm. Like Ogilvie, they found that perceptions of HRM practices

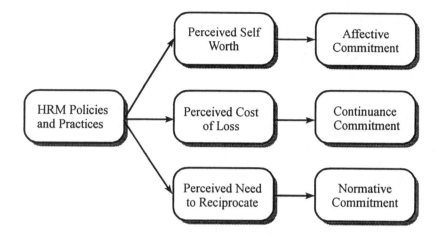

Figure 5.1. HRM practice and commitment: A simplified process model

contributed over and above context factors (supervisor relations, participation in decision making, and communication) in explaining differences in commitment. Actual promotion rate and length of service were also found to be positively related to commitment. On the basis of these findings, Gaertner and Nollen concluded that "psychological commitment is higher among employees who believe they are being treated as resources to be developed rather than commodities to buy and sell" (p. 987).

It appears from the results of these early studies that employees' affective commitment to the organization is indeed related to their perceptions of HRM practices. In what follows, we review the results of more recent research and discuss their implications for "managing for commitment." We begin by considering studies linking commitment to HRM practices, actual or perceived, in the areas of recruitment and selection, socialization and training, assessment and promotion, and compensation and benefits. In these studies, specific HRM practices are considered individually. We follow this with an examination of studies focusing on integrated HRM systems.

Recruitment and Selection

Typically, recruitment and selection processes are closely aligned in practice, and therefore we consider them together here. At issue is whether organizations can do anything during recruitment and selection that will influence or set the stage for subsequent commitment. For example, will the way individuals are treated as applicants affect the likelihood of their becoming committed employees? Is it possible to select from among applicants those who are most likely to become committed employees?

Probably the most widely studied attribute of organizational recruitment practices is accuracy of the information provided to recruits. Wanous (1980, 1992) contrasted two approaches to recruitment: the traditional "hard sell" approach and one in which organizations provide realistic job previews that describe both positive and negative aspects of jobs. He argued that, by using realistic job previews, organizations can increase the job satisfaction, (affective) organizational commitment, and job survival of new hires without having a negative impact on productivity. Meta-analytic reviews of realistic job preview research provide some support for these claims (e.g., McEvoy & Cascio, 1985; Premack & Wanous, 1985). Although the overall effect of realistic job previews on commitment was quite modest, evidence did suggest that the strength of the effect varied across studies (Premack & Wanous) and therefore might depend on how and under what conditions realistic job previews are used.

To better understand *when* realistic job previews are likely to influence commitment (and related attitudes), it is important to consider *why* they do. Several theoretical explanations have been offered (see Breaugh, 1983; Wanous, 1980, 1992; Wanous & Colella, 1989). First, when companies provide accurate information, applicants are better able to determine whether the job will meet their specific needs. Consequently, those who continue in the selection process and accept job offers should be more likely to find the jobs satisfying. Second, by lowering applicants' expectations, it is less likely that these expectations will be disconfirmed once they enter the organization. Third, those who are informed about the less desirable aspects of their future jobs will have the opportunity to prepare themselves and find ways to cope with problems if they encounter them. Yet a fourth possibility is that, being confronted with both the pros and cons of a job option, applicants become more aware of the choice they have to make (e.g., accept or reject; this job or another). Individuals who freely chose a course of action are likely to be more committed to it (Kiesler, 1971; Salancik, 1977a). Finally, organizations that are willing to be honest with applicants, even at the risk of losing potentially valuable employees, might be perceived as more trustworthy and supportive than those that use a hard-sell approach. The reader might notice considerable similarity between these explanations and the mechanisms presumed to be involved in the development of affective commitment (see Chapter 4).

Far less attention has been given to examining the process by which realistic job previews exert their effects than to examining the effects themselves (Breaugh, 1983). Nevertheless, recognizing that these mechanisms might be operating gives some clues as to when their use might be most likely to influence commitment. For example, realistic job previews should have their strongest effects (a) with inexperienced applicants who are likely to have unrealistic expectations, (b) when economic conditions are such that applicants are not "forced" to take jobs even if the jobs do not meet the applicants' needs, and (c) when aspects of the job are truly negative and might require special coping mechanisms (cf. Breaugh; Wanous, 1980).

These findings, then, suggest recruiting strategies that the organization can use to at least set the stage for the development of commitment. What about "selecting" for commitment? In theory, this might be possible, but the evidence is not sufficient to draw firm conclusions. As noted in Chapter 4, Mowday et al. (1982) argued that new employees might vary in their "propensity" to become committed. Moreover, these authors identified three broad categories of variables that together determine propensity: (a) personal characteristics (e.g., previous experience, desire to establish a career in an organization, self-efficacy), (b) preentry expectations, and (c) organizational choice variables (e.g., volition, irrevocability). The propensity hypothesis has been tested in two studies (Lee et al., 1992; Pierce & Dunham, 1987), and both reported that propensity, measured prior to entry into the organization, predicted subsequent commitment. Lee et al. also found some evidence to suggest that propensity might influence commitment by shaping the way employees perceive their early experiences; those with a higher propensity for commitment tended to view the same objective experiences more positively than did those with lower propensity.

One difficulty in interpreting these findings from the standpoint of whether one can select employees who are predisposed to becoming committed stems from the complexity of the propensity construct as defined and measured. It is not clear from the findings reported by Pierce and Dunham (1987) or Lee et al. (1992) which of the various components of propensity are responsible for the correlation with commitment. Only one of the components—personal characteristics—is really relevant to the selection issue. The others—preentry expectations and choice variables—are more likely to be influenced during the recruitment and selection processes, as we discussed above in the context of realistic job previews. Thus, until it can be demonstrated that specific demographic or dispositional variables associated with commitment propensity contribute to its influence on subsequent commitment, there is no basis for its use in selection decisions.

One final note on the issue of propensity. Although the focus of both theory and research to date has been primarily on propensity for affective commitment, it is also possible that individuals will differ in their propensity for normative and continuance commitment. We noted in Chapter 4, for example, that Meyer et al. (1993) found that individual differences in a generalized "sense of obligation" correlated significantly with nurses' continuance and normative commitment to both their organizations and the nursing profession. Meyer et al. (in press) found a positive correlation between the importance of comfort and security measured prior to organizational entry and continuance commitment measured during the first year of employment. This finding suggests some advantage to taking a somewhat broader focus in future research on commitment propensity.

Socialization and Training

One way that an organization might hope to build on employees' initial predisposition for commitment is through socialization and training. Investigation of the effects of socialization practices on commitment was facilitated by Van Maanen and Schein (1979), who devised a six-dimensional classification scheme (see Table 5.1), and Jones (1986), who developed a set of measures to determine where along these dimensions an organization's socialization practices fall. These measures have been used in several studies, and the evidence clearly indicates a link between perceived socialization experiences and commitment (e.g., Allen & Meyer, 1990b; Ashforth & Saks, 1996; Baker & Feldman, 1990; Jones, 1986; Mignerey, Rubin, & Gorden, 1995).

The dimension that has consistently been found to have the strongest association with commitment is *investiture versus divestiture* (e.g., Allen & Meyer, 1990b; Ashforth & Saks, 1996; Jones, 1986). The investiture-divestiture dimension, as measured by Jones's instrument, reflects "the degree to which newcomers receive positive [investiture] or negative [divestiture] support after entry from experienced organizational members" (p. 265). Commitment tends to be stronger when organizations use investiture as opposed to divestiture tactics. Thus, reinforcing newcomers' sense of self-worth and providing a supportive environment appears to be a more effective strategy for instilling a strong sense of commitment than one designed to break down and reshape newcomers' self-image (see Van Maanen & Schein, 1979, for a more detailed description of these strategies).

Instilling commitment is only one of several objectives that organizations attempt to achieve through socialization. A somewhat disconcerting finding re-

TABLE 5.1 Van Maanen and Schein's (1979) Six Dimensions of Organizational Socialization

Formal		*Informal*
Recruits are segregated from other organizational members during socialization.	vs.	Recruits are integrated with other organizational members during socialization.
Collective		*Individual*
Recruits are grouped together and receive common socialization experiences.	vs.	Recruits receive unique socialization experiences.
Sequential		*Random*
The organization specifies a fixed progression of steps for the career to follow.	vs.	Careers follow an unknown or continually changing series of steps in the organization.
Fixed		*Variable*
Recruits are provided with the expected time line for completing each stage of their career.	vs.	Recruits are provided with little or no information concerning the expected completion of career stages.
Serial		*Disjunctive*
An experienced job incumbent facilitates the socialization of new recruits by serving as a role model.	vs.	Socialization is conducted without the assistance of experienced job incumbents.
Investiture		*Divestiture*
The organization acknowledges and supports all personal characteristics of the recruit.	vs.	The organization ignores, discourages, and/or attempts to change personal characteristics of the recruit.

ported by Jones (1986), therefore, was that the socialization practices associated with higher levels of commitment tend to be negatively associated with employees' self-reported tendency to be innovative in the way they perform their roles. Moreover, commitment itself was found to correlate negatively with orientation toward innovation. These findings might be of particular concern to organizations wanting to foster in their employees both a high level of commitment and a willingness to innovate.

Fortunately, more recent research has demonstrated that the negative correlation between commitment and innovation is relatively weak and that the socialization dimensions that have the strongest influence on commitment and role innovation are different (Allen & Meyer, 1990b; Ashforth & Saks, 1996). For example, Allen and Meyer found that role innovation was most strongly related to variation on the *serial versus disjunctive* dimension; innovation was greater when a disjunctive strategy was used. Nevertheless, Jones's (1986) finding should sensitize practitioners to the fact that their efforts to achieve one objective through socialization could have other unintended, and possibly undesirable, effects.

Although these findings have potentially important implications for the design of socialization programs, limitations of the research raise questions about their generalizability. For example, tests of Van Maanen and Schein's (1979) model have been conducted largely with highly educated newcomers (e.g., MBAs) during the first year of employment (Ashforth & Saks, 1996; for an exception, see Baker & Feldman, 1990). It is unclear to what extent these findings are representative of what would be found with less educated or more heterogeneous samples or for socialization conducted during later career stages. Moreover, research has focused largely on the *form* of socialization without concern for the *content*.

It might well be that the message conveyed to employees during socialization is more important in determining their commitment than are the structural charac-teristics of the practices (cf. Ashforth & Saks, 1996; Pascale, 1985). Chao, O'Leary-Kelly, Wolf, Klein, and Gardner (1994) developed a method of clas-sifying socialization content that might be useful in testing this hypothesis. Specifically, they identified six content areas that are potentially subject to direct influence by organizations through their socialization practices: performance proficiency, politics, language, people, organizational goal and values, and history. It is possible that socialization programs designed to familiarize employees with organizational goals and values will have a positive impact on affective commit-ment regardless of how they are conducted (e.g., individually or in groups, formally or informally). It is also possible that socialization will be more effective in fostering commitment if the content is appropriate to career stage (Ostroff & Kozlowski, 1992). For example, new hires might be influenced most by informa-tion that helps them understand their role and become competent at their task (performance proficiency); experienced employees might be influenced more by information of relevance to upward movement (e.g., politics). Finally, little attempt has been made to determine how these organization-initiated socialization prac-tices interact with employees' own information-seeking strategies (see Morrison, 1993; Ostroff & Kozlowski; Wanous & Colella, 1989) to influence commitment and other outcome variables.

Training is often an important part of the socialization process. Although commitment might not be the intended, or at least the most obvious, objective of training, it can nevertheless be influenced in the process. This fact was demonstrated in a study conducted by Tannenbaum, Mathieu, Salas, and Cannon-Bowers (1991). They assessed the commitment of recruits immediately on arrival at a U.S. Naval Training Command for an 8-week socialization-type training process and again following training. They found that, overall, organizational commitment increased following training. Moreover, posttraining organizational commitment was positively associated with perceptions of training fulfillment (the extent to which the training fulfilled trainees' expectations and desires), satisfaction with the training experience, and training performance. Saks (1995) obtained similar results in a study conducted with a sample of newly hired entry-level accountants. Moreover, he found that the effects of training on commitment were attributable, in part, to its effects on newcomers' feelings of self-efficacy (perceptions of their ability to perform the required task). This latter finding is consistent with the argument made in Chapter 4 that feelings of competence play a role in the development of affective commitment.

Tannenbaum et al. (1991) also found some evidence that organizational commitment may have reciprocal effects on training success. They found a strong positive correlation between commitment and employees' motivation for training, a variable that was found to be an important predictor of training satisfaction and performance. This finding has been replicated in a large-scale study of government supervisory and management personnel (Facteau, Dobbins, Russell, Ladd, & Kudisch, 1995). Thus, although more research is necessary, existing evidence suggests that commitment can be affected by training experiences and can, in turn, influence employees' motivation for future training.

Assessment and Promotion

Policies and practices concerning the movement of employees, particularly upward movement, once the employees are in the organization might also be expected to have an impact on their commitment. As noted earlier, Gaertner and Nollen (1989) found that commitment was higher among employees who had been promoted and was also related to employees' perceptions that the company had a policy of promoting from within. Such a policy might be perceived by employees as evidence that the organization is committed to them, which leads them to reciprocate.

Obviously, not everyone within an organization will be promoted. This raises the question, then, of how promotion decisions might influence the commitment of those who are, and even more interestingly those who are not, promoted. Robertson, Iles, Gratton, and Sharpley (1991) examined the impact of a management development and tiering program used by a large financial services organization to evaluate employees in early- and mid-career. They found that commitment and turnover intentions were strongly influenced by the outcome of early-career assessments; those who received negative feedback became less committed and more likely to consider leaving the company. Reactions to assessments conducted in mid-career (early 30s), however, were affected more by the perceived adequacy of the assessment procedures involved than by the outcome. Thus, the type of strategy needed to maintain commitment among those employees given negative feedback might depend on their career stage.

Schwarzwald, Koslowsky, and Shalit (1992) examined the effect of promotion decisions on the commitment of a group of Israeli employees who had declared their candidacy for promotion. Those who were promoted were subsequently more committed than those who were not. The latter also perceived greater inequity in the decision-making process and tended to be absent more frequently following the decision. Schwarzwald et al. suggested that the difference in equity perceptions was probably because all those who declared their candidacy for promotion believed they qualified; a negative decision, therefore, was inconsistent with their own beliefs.

Finally, Fletcher (1991) found that the commitment of managerial candidates in a major U.K. bank who went through assessment centers changed little in preassessment, postassessment, and follow-up surveys. Moreover, successful and unsuccessful candidates differed little in commitment either before or after the assessment. Performance in the assessment center did, however, affect candidates in other ways (e.g., self-esteem). On the basis of the findings of the studies described above, it is possible that the absence of an effect on commitment was because of perceptions that the assessments, even when undesirable, were fair.

Together, these findings suggest that a policy of promotion from within can have a beneficial effect on commitment, perhaps because it conveys a commitment on behalf of the organization to the development of employees' careers (Gaertner & Nollen, 1989). Among those who are considered for promotion, the outcome of the decision is likely to have an effect on commitment, but for some (e.g., those in mid-career), the perception of fairness in the decision-making process might be even more important. In the light of these findings, it is important that organizations communicate clearly how their decisions were made and why those who did not receive a promotion were passed over. Schwarzwald et al. (1992) noted that it should not be assumed that those who seek promotion will be "prepared" for rejection and accept it gracefully.

It is also interesting to consider the potential impact that failure to receive a promotion might have on other forms of commitment. Although affective commitment might weaken, continuance commitment could increase, particularly for more senior employees who view their options outside the organization as limited. Consistent with this possibility, Meyer et al. (1989) found that continuance commitment was greater among managers who were rated by their superiors as less promotable. Organizations might not be concerned about a decline in affective commitment of those they pass over if they believe that these individuals will seek employment elsewhere. If the decline in affective commitment is accompanied by an increase in continuance commitment, however, the organization might find that it is retaining employees who are not highly motivated to do more than is required in order to keep their jobs until retirement. It would be wise, therefore, to find ways to maintain the affective commitment of these employees or to provide them with assistance in gaining opportunities elsewhere.

Compensation and Benefits

Although relatively scant attention has been given to examining the effects of the administration of salary and benefits on commitment, one compensation-relevant practice that has received some attention is the use of an employee stock ownership plan (ESOP). ESOPs are increasing in popularity for several reasons, including the belief that employees who have a stake in the company will be more committed to it (Klein, 1987). Indeed, evidence for a link between organizational commitment and ESOPs (and related systems) has been obtained in several studies (e.g., Buchko, 1992, 1993; Florkowski & Schuster, 1992; Klein; Klein & Hall, 1988; Tucker, Nock, & Toscano, 1989; Wetzel & Gallagher, 1990). Many of these studies also addressed the issue of *why* ESOPs are related to commitment.

Klein (1987) identified three models that have been used to explain the link between employee ownership and commitment. According to the first of these— the *intrinsic satisfaction model*—commitment derives directly from ownership and should therefore be proportional to the amount of stock an employee holds. The *extrinsic satisfaction model* proposes that commitment will be proportional to the degree of financial gain the employee realizes (or has the potential to realize) as a function of holding stock in the company. Finally, according to the *instrumental satisfaction model,* employee ownership is believed to increase commitment because it increases the actual or perceived influence that employees have in decision making within the organization. Using data from more than 2,800 ESOP participants from 37 companies, Klein found some support for both the extrinsic and instrumental satisfaction models but not for the intrinsic satisfaction model.

More recent studies have provided mixed support for the instrumental satisfaction and extrinsic satisfaction models; the intrinsic satisfaction model continues to have scant support. For example, Buchko (1993) found that financial value of the ESOP was indirectly related to commitment through its influence on overall satisfaction with the plan. In contrast, perceived influence resulting from ownership was found to be directly related to both satisfaction with the plan and commitment to the organization. In a quasi-experimental study, Tucker et al. (1989) found that organizational commitment increased following the introduction of an ESOP in a small clothing store but that perceived influence did not change. Interestingly, they found that the commitment of both participants and nonparticipants increased following the introduction of the ESOP, and they speculated that this finding might have been a result of a general change in the climate of the organization. Finally, in a study designed to examine the influence of profit sharing on commitment, Florkowski and Schuster (1992) found that concerns about the financial implications of the plan (performance-reward contingency, pay equity) were related to support for the plan, which in turn was an important determinant of organizational commitment. Perceived influence was not directly related to plan support, as had been anticipated, but did relate to commitment indirectly through its influence on job satisfaction.

Together, these findings suggest that the introduction of an ESOP alone is not sufficient to increase affective commitment. Employees will expect to benefit either financially or in terms of their ability to influence decisions or both. If increasing commitment is an objective, it would appear that making the plan financially meaningful and/or increasing employees' opportunity to participate in decision making should be an important part of the plan. With regard to financial meaningfulness, however, it must be kept in mind that too much emphasis on this factor could actually reduce affective commitment (cf. Caldwell et al., 1990) or lead to the development of other forms of commitment. For example, an ESOP that requires that employees stay for a fixed period of time in order to receive the organization's contribution to the plan can increase the cost of leaving the organization (continuance commitment). In sum, the implementation of ESOPs must be undertaken with care. Numerous factors (e.g., management philosophy, system design, contextual origin) can influence the success of ESOPs, including its influence on commitment (see Pierce & Furo, 1990, for a more complete discussion and set of recommendations).

Even less research has examined the impact of benefits on commitment. Nevertheless, the administration of benefits could conceivably have implications for employee commitment. Consider, for example, the potential impact of organizations' efforts to respond to the increase in the number of families in which both parents work by providing "family-responsive benefits" (e.g., flexible hours, day care assistance). Goldberg, Greenberger, Koch-Jones, O'Neil, and Hamill (1989) found a positive correlation between satisfaction with such family-responsive benefits and the commitment of employed parents of preschool-age children (married fathers and married and single mothers). Moreover, they found that a substantial percentage of the employees surveyed said they would change employers to receive such benefits. In a more recent study, Grover and Crooker (1995), using data collected in a national survey of more than 1,500 U.S. workers, found a positive correlation between availability of family-responsive benefits and affective commitment. They argued that organizations that offer such benefits are perceived by employees as showing greater caring and concern (organizational support) and as being fair in their dealings with employees.

Grover and Crooker (1995) noted that the correlations between benefit availability and commitment were not large and that there may be limits to the generalizability of their results. For example, they suggested that the introduction of family-responsive benefits should be consistent with the existing climate of the organization. If employees view these benefits as having been introduced in response to external pressure or as a token gesture, the benefits may have less impact (cf. Koys, 1988, 1991). Moreover, Grover and Crooker's explanation for their findings assumes that a norm for need-based distribution of resources exists; if the norm is for equity-based distribution, the provision of benefits that meet the needs of a select group of employees might create some resentment.

HRM Systems

The findings reported above suggest that HRM practices do have the potential to influence employees' commitment. We discuss the implications and limitations of this research in more detail below. One limitation of the research, however, we elaborate on here. Although studying the effects of specific HRM practices individually has advantages, in reality they do not operate in isolation. To the contrary, organizations develop complex HRM systems made up of component parts that, ideally, operate in unison and are compatible with their overall business strategy (Huselid, 1995; MacDuffie, 1995; Snell & Youndt, 1995; Wright &

McMahan, 1992). It is possible, therefore, that the correlation we observe between any particular HRM practice (e.g., use of realistic job previews, investiture strategies of socialization) and commitment does not reflect a causal effect of that strategy, but rather reflects its association with other practices, HRM systems, or general business strategies that do exert causal effects. One way to address this problem is to examine the effects of intact HRM systems.

An essential requirement for both theory and research from a systems perspective is a meaningful way of classifying HRM systems (Arthur, 1994); that is, it is necessary to be able to differentiate among integrated systems of HRM practices in terms of their basic approaches or objectives in managing human resources and to relate the use of these different systems to relevant outcomes. Although various typologies have been suggested (e.g., Dyer & Holder, 1988; Miles & Snow, 1984; Osterman, 1987; Schuler & Jackson, 1987), our discussion here focuses on "control" and "commitment" strategies (Arthur, 1992, 1994; Lawler, 1986; Walton, 1985). As suggested by their labels, these strategies differ in terms of the value placed on achieving organizational objectives through the establishment of a committed workforce. Arthur (1994, p. 672) contrasted the two approaches as follows:

> Control and commitment represent two distinct approaches to shaping employees' behaviors and attitudes at work. The goal of control of human resource systems is to reduce direct labor costs, or improve efficiency, by enforcing employee compliance with specific rules and procedures and basing employee rewards on some measurable output criteria (Eisenhardt, 1985; Walton, 1985). In contrast, commitment human resource systems shape desired employee behaviors and attitudes by forging psychological links between organizational and employee goals. In other words, the focus is on developing committed employees who can be trusted to use their discretion to carry out job tasks in ways that are consistent with organizational goals.

Arthur (1994) compared the relative effectiveness of these two systems in a study conducted with 30 U.S. steel minimills. Using data obtained from human resource managers in these minimills, he classified their HRM systems as reflecting a commitment or control orientation. In contrast with control systems, commitment systems were characterized by greater decentralization in quality- and cost-control activities, more general training and development, higher overall wages, and a lower percentage of average employment costs accounted for by bonuses and incentive payments. Arthur then compared these minimills in terms of manufacturing performance (labor efficiency and scrap rate) and turnover rate. Minimills using commitment strategies were found to have significantly higher performance and lower turnover, compared with those using control strategies.

In a study conducted by using data obtained from surveys of 62 automotive plants from around the world, MacDuffie (1995) found that the use of high-commitment HRM practices (focus on openness to learning and interpersonal skills in selection, compensation contingent on plant performance, low status differential, and extensive training) was associated with higher levels of productivity and quality, particularly when appropriately integrated with work systems (e.g., use of work teams, employee involvement in quality control) and production strategies. On the basis of his findings, MacDuffie emphasized the importance of developing "bundles" of HRM practices that are internally consistent (mutually reinforcing) and compatible with the broader "organizational logic."

In another system-based study, Huselid (1995) examined the relations between the use of what he called "high performance work practices" and various indices of corporate performance. HRM professionals in 968 firms provided data concerning their HRM practices (e.g., recruitment, selection, incentive compensation, labor management participation). Although he did not classify organizations as employing a commitment or control system per se, the work practices he measured correspond quite closely to those included in a commitment system as described by Arthur (1994). He found that the use of these practices was associated with lower levels of turnover and higher levels of productivity and corporate financial success.

Although the amount of research conducted from a systems approach is admittedly limited, the findings do provide some support for the argument that organizations using HRM practices designed to foster commitment will have lower turnover rates, more productive employees, and greater overall success (Walton, 1985). The reader may have noticed, however, that missing from this research is an assessment of employee commitment. Consequently, we cannot conclude with certainty that the HRM practices intended to foster commitment actually did so and that the impact of these practices on turnover and productivity is attributable to the increase in commitment.

Taken together, the results of research using the systems approach and focusing on individual HRM practices suggest that organizations can influence their employees' commitment and their bottom lines through their HRM policies and practices. We examine the implications of these findings in more detail following a discussion of management practices under conditions of change.

Management of Change

In this section, we examine how employees' commitment is affected by major changes taking place in organizations today. We focus primarily on the impact of downsizing because it has been studied most extensively. Moreover, many specific changes associated with downsizing (e.g., reduction in the size of the workforce, changes in duties and responsibilities) are also involved in other forms of reorganization (e.g., merger/acquisition, reengineering). Consequently, much of what has been learned in the study of downsizing can be applied to understanding reactions to these other forms of change.

Organizational downsizing is occurring with increasing regularity. It has been estimated, for example, that approximately 90% of large organizations in North America reduced their workforce in recent years (Emshoff, 1994). Advocates view downsizing as a legitimate response to increased competition and the need for greater efficiency; critics view it as a shortsighted attempt to improve the bottom line or as another management fad. Whatever the motive, many experts believe that the anticipated economic benefits (e.g., reduced expenses, higher profits, increased return on investments, increased stock prices) and organizational benefits (e.g., lower overhead, smoother communication, greater entrepreneurship, increased productivity) of downsizing often do not materialize (Cameron, 1994; Cascio, 1993; O'Neill & Lenn, 1995). Of course, many factors determine whether downsizing achieves or fails to achieve its objectives. We focus here on how downsizing affects those who remain after the cuts and how the reactions of these "survivors" (particularly their commitment) contribute to the success of the downsizing organization.

Downsizing has the potential to influence affective, continuance, and normative commitment. Certainly, organizations hope that downsizing can be accomplished without reducing the affective attachment of those who remain to carry out their mission; some might even hope to enhance commitment by convincing employees that their jobs have been "enriched." Indeed, downsizing more often than not involves reductions in the management ranks and thereby creates the potential for increased responsibility among the nonmanagerial employees. The uncertainty created by downsizing, however, might also make salient to survivors what they stand to lose should they be victims in the next round of cuts. This focus on costs can increase employees' continuance commitment. Finally, survivors might feel grateful for having been spared in the cuts and develop a stronger sense of obligation, or normative commitment, to the company. Moreover, the guilt that some remaining employees experience as part of the "survivor syndrome" (Cascio,

1993) might be translated into a sense of obligation to work harder to justify the decision to retain them.

As organizations reduce their number of employees, they rely more than ever on those who remain to do what is needed for the organization to survive and be successful. Thus, they need to retain employees who are qualified and willing to take on the added tasks and responsibilities of those who have left. Tasks may become less well defined, and employees will be expected to find creative ways to improve their efficiency. With a leaner workforce, absenteeism and tardiness become serious problems, and turnover, particularly of top performers, can be devastating.

Some evidence suggests that employees often do not fulfill their employers' expectations following downsizing. Brockner, DeWitt, Grover, and Reed (1990) found that survivors report they sometimes exert less effort as layoffs occur. Greenhalgh and Jick (1979) found that turnover is a problem following layoff and that, frequently, layoffs result in increased turnover among the firm's most valued employees. In a similar vein, Mone (1994) found that those who were most confident in their abilities were most likely to consider leaving the organization following a downsizing—presumably because these employees viewed them-selves as having the greatest opportunity to find alternative employment outside the organization (had the lowest continuance commitment). These findings illustrate the importance of identifying the factors that influence the post-layoff commitment of survivors. A number of studies have been conducted to this end.

In a study of employees in a chain of retail outlets, Brockner, Grover, Reed, DeWitt, and O'Malley (1987) found that downsizing had the most negative impact on commitment when survivors had close personal and/or working relationships with the layoff victims and when they did not think the victims had been given adequate support or compensation (e.g., generous severance pay, help in relocating inside or outside the organization). Davy, Kinicki, and Scheck (1991) found that post-layoff commitment was positively related to the perceived fairness of the layoff decision and to feelings of job security.

Interestingly, Davy et al. (1991) found that perceptions of the fairness of layoff decisions were positively related to employees' perceptions of the fairness of organizational decisions in the past. Although the researchers did not measure commitment prior to the layoff when these earlier decisions were made, on the basis of the justice research reviewed in Chapter 4, one might suspect that employees who had been treated fairly in the past would be more affectively committed to the organization. Perhaps this commitment led the employees to view the layoff decisions as fair. If so, there is reason to expect that the negative impact of downsizing will be weaker when commitment is initially high. Consistent with this line of reasoning, Greenhalgh, McKersie, and Gilkey (1986) argued that having a committed workforce makes it easier for companies to elicit cooperation in difficult times, and they gave examples of how this principle has been put to practice at IBM.

Brockner, Tyler, and Cooper-Schneider (1992) addressed this issue empirically by measuring commitment prior to layoff and examining its effect, along with perceptions of the fairness of the layoff, on post-layoff commitment. Interestingly, they found that the greatest reduction in commitment and work effort following downsizing was among those who were previously most committed but who thought the layoff decisions were unfair (e.g., based on politics rather than on merit). Thus, it appears that having a committed workforce prior to downsizing does not guarantee that survivors will accept the organization's decision and maintain their commitment. In fact, these employees might be most disillusioned if they do not view the downsizing process as fair.

As we noted above, organizations wishing to maintain a high level of affective commitment among their remaining employees might hope that these employees would view the changes to their own jobs (e.g., increased workload and responsibility) as "enrichment." Brockner, Weisenfeld, Reed, Grover, and Martin (1993) examined the relation between survivors' perceptions of the intrinsic quality of their jobs and their commitment following layoff and found that it was moderated by perceptions of the context of the layoff. Specifically, they found a stronger association between job quality and post-layoff commitment among those employees who thought that (a) the layoff decisions were fair and (b) their coworkers viewed the layoff positively.

It is clear from these findings that perceptions of fairness of the layoff decisions are important in determining post-layoff commitment. How are these perceptions shaped? The downsizing organization itself can have an impact on these perceptions through its communication with employees prior to, during, and following the downsizing efforts. Although the impact of communication processes has not been studied extensively, recent findings do bear on this issue. Brockner et al. (1990) examined the influence of managerial explanations for the downsizing on survivor commitment. They found that adequate explanations provided by managers mitigated the negative impact of layoffs on organizational commitment, particularly among employees who were uncertain about why the layoffs occurred and who feared further layoffs. Mellor (1992) also found that explanations for a layoff can have an impact on commitment, but in this case, commitment to the union was affected. Employees were less committed to their union when they accepted the organization's explanation that the union was responsible for the need to downsize. Unfortunately, Mellor did not measure organizational commitment, so it is not possible to determine what effect attempts to deflect blame had on employees' reactions to the organization, particularly when the explanation was not accepted. Nevertheless, the findings do suggest that employees' reactions will be influenced by their attributions of causality for the layoff. Just as commitment to the union declined among those who saw the union as responsible, commitment to the organization might be expected to decline among those who consider the organization responsible.

In sum, then, the affective commitment of survivors of downsizing can play an important role in shaping the success of the initiative. Indeed, as Cameron (1994) pointed out, the fact that downsizing often fails to meet its long-term objectives could be in large measure because of the adverse effects it has on the commitment of survivors.

> Implementing a workforce reduction strategy may be necessary as a severe economic hardship is encountered, of course, but the short-term payoffs are usually negated by long-term costs. The violation of the implicit employment contract between the organization and its employees leads to a loss of loyalty and commitment among the workforce and a deterioration in willingness to go the extra mile on behalf of the company. (p. 199)

Fortunately, however, it appears that the commitment of survivors can be maintained through the careful development and implementation of a reduction strategy. The research findings reviewed above suggest that perceptions of fairness in the treatment of both victims and survivors play an important role in determining commitment. Strategies designed to enhance perceptions of fairness, therefore, are more likely to result in long-term success (see Cameron, 1994; Ford & Perrewé, 1993).

Like downsizing, mergers and acquisitions are occurring with increasing regularity in North America and abroad. It was estimated that, between 1983 and 1986, more than 12,000 mergers and acquisitions involving more than $490 billion took place in the United States ("For Better or Worse", 1987). Although the downturn in the economy in the early 1990s led to a decline in mergers and acquisitions, Cartwright and Cooper (1993, 1994) observed that activity has begun to pick up again, with the number of mergers and acquisitions in the first 6 months of 1993 showing an increase of 30% over the same period in the previous year.

Much has been written about the potential consequences of mergers and acquisitions, and there is no shortage of examples of failures (see Buono & Bowditch, 1989). One anticipated negative consequence of a merger or acquisition is a reduction of commitment, particularly among members of the acquired firm or the smaller of the merging companies. Only a few studies have been conducted, however, to identify the factors that contribute to the decline in commitment or, alternatively, help maintain commitment at a high level. This lack is perhaps because mergers and acquisitions tend, for various reasons, to be arranged in relative secrecy (Newman & Krzystofiak, 1993). Nevertheless, those studies that have been conducted have generated some interesting results. We briefly review two of these studies.

Schweiger and DeNisi (1991) speculated that the negative impact of mergers on employees' commitment might be because, at least in part, of the misinformation (usually negative) spread in the absence of clear communication on the part of management about how the merger will affect employees. They conducted a quasi-experimental study in one of two merging Fortune 500 companies to test the hypothesis that providing employees with a "realistic merger preview" (analogous to realistic job preview, discussed earlier) would lessen the decline in commitment. Employees in one plant were given information about the merger shortly after it was announced and were kept informed about the progress being made thereafter through face-to-face meetings and a company newsletter. A hotline was also set up to address questions as they arose. Employees in a second plant were not provided with this information. The researchers found that whereas commitment in the second plant declined steadily after the announcement, commitment in the plant where previews were given remained close to pre-announcement levels.

Newman and Krzystofiak (1993) conducted a longitudinal field study to examine the impact of an acquisition on the commitment of employees in the target firm (a small U.S. bank). They found, as expected, that commitment declined following the announcement of the acquisition. Not all employees were equally affected, however. The investigators noted that the decline in commitment was accompanied by more negative perceptions of the job and lower satisfaction with supervision. Although their data did not permit them to address issues of causality, Newman and Krzystofiak speculated that dissatisfaction with the change in jobs and supervision was responsible for the decline in commitment. Job security did not appear to be a factor in determining commitment in this case, but might be in others. Like Schweiger and DeNisi (1991), Newman and Krzystofiak noted that communication is likely to be an important component in any program designed to build commitment to the new organization.

Although the findings of both of these studies suggest that accurate communication is important, there may be limitations to how much information can or should be provided (Hogan & Overmyer-Day, 1994). Nevertheless, if companies involved in mergers and acquisitions want their employees to maintain a high level of commitment and desire to work toward the success of the new organization, they need to recognize the concerns that employees will inevitably have. If communication is not a viable strategy for addressing these concerns, other options will have to be tried. By understanding the mechanisms involved in the development and maintenance of commitment (see Chapter 4), it should be possible to identify such options. As we saw in the case of downsizing, perceptions of justice are likely to play an important role.

Summary and Implications

The research findings we have reviewed in this chapter should be viewed with cautious optimism. The reason for caution is that the methods used in this research have several limitations. First, most studies used cross-sectional designs that are of limited value in establishing cause and effect. Second, HRM practices were often assessed by using surveys completed by employees themselves; concerns over accuracy aside, obtaining measures of both practices and commitment from the same source can lead to inflation of the observed correlations (e.g., because of common errors in ratings). Third, as we noted earlier, when examined in isolation, a particular HRM practice might be found to relate to commitment because of its association with other (unmeasured) HRM practices or business strategies that are the true causes of commitment.

These limitations aside, the reason for optimism is that the findings that have been obtained are generally consistent with theory, as well as with anecdotal evidence and case-study results reported in the popular press and trade/business journals (e.g., Buller, 1988; Caudron, 1993; Feldman & Leana, 1989; Leonard, 1992). Although we still caution against placing too much faith in the results of any one study, by examining the findings concerning a specific management practice obtained in one setting in the context of the broader theoretical and empirical literature on the development of commitment (see Chapter 4), it is possible to speculate on how that practice might affect commitment in other settings. It is also possible to speculate on how practices not yet examined empirically might affect commitment. For example, a common theme in explanations offered for many of the findings, particularly those involving practices that had important implications for employees' careers and personal well-being (e.g., promotion, downsizing), was the importance of fairness. We might also expect perceptions of fairness to mediate the influence of other HRM practices, such as performance appraisal, affirmative action, incentive-payment plans, and drug-testing programs, on commitment. In Chapter 4, we discussed mechanisms believed to be involved in the development of affective commitment. Companies wanting to design HRM systems that, among other things, help foster stronger commitment among their employees should consider how the various practices within the system, individually and in combination, are likely to influence these mechanisms.

It must be emphasized that specific practices do not operate in isolation. Rather, to have the intended effect on commitment, organizational policies and practices must be consistent with one another, with the overall business strategy, and with the existing culture of the organization (cf. Guzzo & Noonan, 1994). We noted earlier, for example, that the introduction of child care benefits is unlikely to have a positive effect on employees, other than those it benefits directly, in a culture that emphasizes an equity-based reward system. Indeed, the introduction of such a benefit package might have exactly the opposite effect in this case. Similarly, open and honest communication during a merger cannot be expected to buffer the negative impact of the change if the climate in existence at the time is one of secrecy and mistrust.

Another important consideration in attempting to foster commitment through HRM practices is that *perception* is more important than reality. Employees will react to conditions as they perceive them. This can lead to situations where a policy or practice has unexpected, and possibly undesirable, consequences. Iles, Mabey, and Robertson (1990) provided two good examples of this. First, Sadri, Cooper, and Allison (1989) found that the introduction of stress counseling for postal employees was associated with a reduction in commitment. Similarly, Iles, Robertson, and Rout (1989) found that employees who participated in development centers designed to aid them in career planning and development reported less clear career goals and strategies and were more likely to be thinking of leaving their career field following participation. In both cases, the unexpected outcomes might have resulted from the fact that employees' perceptions were influenced in ways that were quite different from what was intended. For example, participation in stress counseling might have made employees aware that the organization was a major contributor to the stress they were experiencing. Similarly, participation in developmental assessment centers might have increased employees' awareness that they were in the wrong career path (Iles et al., 1990).

A related consideration is the importance of the attributions employees make for an organization's actions. We discussed this in some detail in Chapter 4, but it bears repeating here. Employees are more likely to respond in the desired direction (with increased commitment) to a policy or practice if they believe that the organization was responsible for its introduction and considered employees' interests. For example, Koys (1988, 1991) found that HRM practices were more likely to influence employees' commitment when they were seen as motivated by a concern for employees, rather than by compliance with legal requirements or a desire to increase productivity. Similarly, Kinicki, Carson, and Bohlander (1992) found that perceptions of an organization's commitment to its HRM practices contributed over and above the practices themselves to the prediction of employees' attitudes toward the company and its values. In view of these findings, an alternative explanation for the unexpected outcomes of HRM practices described above might be that employees viewed the counseling programs as having been "imposed" on them in an effort to control rather than to help them. At any rate, the findings once more illustrate the importance of communication in the design and implementation of HRM practices (cf. Guzzo & Noonan, 1994). This communication should include efforts both to inform employees about the intended purpose of the practice and to solicit feedback about employees' perceptions of and reactions to the practice.

Finally, it is important to keep in mind that other forms of commitment can be affected by management practices. As we illustrated in the framework provided at the beginning of this chapter, depending on what mechanisms are activated, a particular practice can lead to higher levels of affective, continuance, or normative commitment. Although the impact of an increase in any one of these components of commitment on employees' intention to remain in the organization might be the same, the effect on their willingness to contribute to the attainment of organizational objectives might not. As you saw in Chapter 3, the most worrisome situation would be one in which a particular practice contributed to an elevation in continuance commitment but not in affective or normative commitment. Employees who remain only because of the costs associated with leaving are unlikely to do more than what is minimally required of them to maintain their jobs. Although companies might not intentionally try to create such a situation, they can do so inadvertently through actions taken to achieve other objectives. For example, a company that uses rapid promotion and generous salaries and benefits to keep its most talented young employees could create a situation in which such employees believe that they are unable to leave even if they have no strong affective attachment to the company. Similarly, companies that focus only on the bottom line as they cut jobs can create a situation in which survivors believe that they are unable to leave, at least until economic conditions improve, but have no desire to remain. These employees are unlikely to be highly motivated to turn the company around.

Multiple Commitments in the Workplace

I n Chapter 2, we argued that to understand commitment at work, one must understand distinctions made with respect to both the *nature* of commitment and the *focus* of commitment; that is, one must recognize that commitment can take multiple forms, each of which can be focused on multiple entities, including the work group, the supervisor, top management, the occupation, and the union. Thus far, we have discussed the development and consequences of affective, continuance, and normative commitment to the organization as a whole. In doing so, we have emphasized the "nature of commitment" distinction while paying much less attention to the "focus of commitment" distinction. Given the volume of organizational commitment research, this emphasis is not at all unreasonable. Nevertheless, it provides a somewhat incomplete picture of work commitment because, clearly, employees can become committed to several work-related domains (Morrow, 1993; Reichers, 1985).

Our objective in this chapter, therefore, is to examine work commitment from a wider perspective. In doing so, we address two somewhat distinct issues. First, we discuss the generalizability, or extension, of the three-component model of commitment to entities other than the organization. Second, we discuss the implications of taking a multiple-foci approach to commitment, with a specific emphasis on issues of compatibility, conflict, and dependencies among the various work-related foci to which people are committed. Because of the considerable potential for confusion regarding terminology, we begin by clarifying some terms that we use in these discussions.

Terminology

Overall, the general terms *foci* and *entities* are used interchangeably to refer to any of the many people, collectives, or activities to which one can become psychologically committed. Accordingly, one's spouse, a volunteer agency, and horseback riding could all be considered foci of one's commitment; in other words, each is an entity to which psychological commitment is possible. Our particular concern, of course, is with work-related entities. Of the several work-related entities to which one can become committed, some can be thought of as "within" and others "outside" the organization. We use the terms *constituencies* to refer to units within a larger organization (e.g., top management, the work group, coworkers, supervisors) and *domains* to refer to those larger bodies (the organization, the union, the occupation or profession). The work organization is not the only domain with constituent parts. For example, a member of a particular union could be committed to several constituencies associated with it: the union steward, the union local, the rank-and-file membership, the national (or international) union, and so on. Finally, consistent with other research, we use the term *multiple commitments,* not to refer to the differences in the *nature* of commitment, but rather to refer collectively to the various *foci* to which a person can become committed. With these terms in mind, we turn to a more substantive discussion of multiple commitments in the workplace.

Generalizability of the Three-Component Conceptualization

The three-component conceptualization of commitment that forms the framework used in this book was developed in an attempt to further our understanding of commitment to the organization. This point should not be taken to suggest, however, that the affective, continuance, and normative commitment constructs need apply only to the organization. Indeed, as indicated in Chapter 2 (see Figure 2.1), it seems quite reasonable to suggest that one could feel affective, continuance, and normative attachment to just about any entity—work-related or otherwise— with which one has a psychological relationship. Using more general (non-organizational) terms, therefore, we could restate our early conceptualization of commitment (Allen & Meyer, 1990a; Meyer & Allen, 1991) as follows:

> Affective, continuance, and normative commitment are psychological states that characterize the person's relationship with the entity in question and have implications for the decision to remain involved with it.

Consider, for example, an individual's psychological commitment to his or her "significant other." Presumably, part of this relationship and the individual's intention to remain in it will be based on emotional attachment to the other person (affective commitment). It is also possible that the individual will recognize costs associated with discontinuing the relationship (continuance commitment). Finally, the individual may also maintain this important interpersonal relationship, to some degree, because of feelings of obligation to the other person (normative commit-ment). Although interesting, the extension of the three-component conceptualiza-tion of commitment to the study of interpersonal relationships is not of direct relevance to this discussion. We use this example primarily to illustrate the point that, in theory, the psychological commitment that a person has to almost any entity could have "want to stay," "have to stay," and "ought to stay" components.

Not a great deal of empirical work has assessed the generalizability of the three-component conceptualization of commitment to other entities within the workplace, although its relevance to the union has been suggested (Kelloway, Catano, & Southwell, 1992). Modified versions of the affective and normative commitment measures developed by Allen and Meyer (1990a) for use in work organizations have been administered by Dunham et al. (1994) to volunteer (nonpaid) members of charitable organizations. (Notice that the focus here was still the organization but that members were volunteers, not employees; also, only two of the three components of commitment were assessed.) Withey (1990) also modified the measures to assess the commitment of university students to their academic program. In neither study is it noted that respondents had any particular difficulty completing the measures; this point suggests that the items assessing the different commitment constructs made sense to the respondents in these contexts. Beyond this, however, little can be inferred about the generalizability of the three-component conceptualization of commitment because neither study was conducted with this as its explicit purpose.

Meyer et al. (1993) attempted to extend the three-component conceptualization to another domain—that of the occupation. The researchers had several reasons for choosing this particular domain. First, it seems clear from other research in this area (e.g., Hall, 1976) that the occupation is psychologically distinct from other work-related entities. Second, the occupation appears to be an entity to which people make psychologically meaningful commitments; that is, although there undoubtedly is variation across people and across occupations, it is obvious that many people take their commitment to their occupational role quite seriously. Third, and related to this, is the intriguing possibility that, in the context of one's work, conflicts arise between the goals and demands of the occupation and those of the organization (Kerr, Von Glinow, & Schriesheim, 1977). Understanding this sort of conflict might arguably be facilitated by a three-component view of occupational commitment. Because this research represents the first extension of the three-component conceptualization of commitment to another work-related domain, it is described here in some detail.

Participants in the Meyer et al. (1993) study came from a single occupation: nursing. Data were collected from two samples, one consisting of student nurses and the other of registered nurses. The first step in this work was to develop measures of affective, continuance, and normative commitment to the occupation that paralleled those used in organizational commitment research. Items written to assess the three forms of commitment to the nursing profession were administered, as part of a larger questionnaire, to the student nurses in all 4 years of a university nursing program. Item selection for each of the three occupational commitment scales involved procedures similar to those used in the development of the measures of affective, continuance, and normative commitment to the organization (Allen & Meyer, 1990a). Following this, the new occupational commitment measures were administered to the registered nurse sample along with measures of affective, continuance, and normative commitment to the organization and several variables that were identified as likely antecedents and consequences of the three forms of occupational commitment and organizational commitment.

Support for a three-component conceptualization of occupational commitment, consistent with that offered for commitment to the organization, came from several analyses conducted by Meyer et al. (1993). First, confirmatory factor analyses of the items making up these three new occupational commitment scales and the three organizational commitment scales were conducted by using the data obtained from registered nurses. Results showed that an oblique six-factor solution (three occupational and three organizational commitment factors) provided the best fit to the data. Second, the pattern of correlations between the new scales and other antecedent variables was generally consistent with expectations. Third, occupational commitment added to the prediction of some outcome variables (e.g., intention to leave nursing, voluntary absence) over and above that explained by the organizational commitment measures. The latter findings are particularly important in the light of concerns of construct redundancy raised by the proliferation of work commitment measures in the literature (Morrow, 1983).

The results of this study can be considered reasonable, albeit preliminary, evidence that the three-component view of commitment can be extended to another domain. Since the development of these measures, they have been administered to at least two other occupational groups—students in the rehabilitation field (Speechley, Noh, & Beggs, 1993) and certified professional accountants (Gross & Fullagar, 1996)—and an occupationally heterogenous sample of government employees (Irving, Coleman, & Cooper, 1996). In the latter two studies, confirmatory factor analyses were conducted on responses to the occupational commitment items; Speechley et al. conducted an exploratory factor analysis. All three studies reported factor analytic results consistent with the idea that occupational commitment has affective, continuance, and normative components. Thus, these studies provide further evidence that the three-component conceptualization of commitment generalizes to the occupational domain.

Thus far, the generalizability of the three-component conceptualization of commitment to other domains (e.g., unions) and to other constituencies within those domains (e.g., the union local, union stewards) has not been tested. It is interesting to speculate, as others have done (Kelloway et al., 1992), whether the three components could be applied successfully to commitment to the union. Like organizational commitment, the conceptualization and operationalization of the union commitment construct have been examined extensively. One dominant measure in the field, developed by Gordon and his colleagues (Gordon, Philpot, Burt, Thompson, & Spiller, 1980), has received considerable psychometric scrutiny and, in the light of this evaluation, has undergone several modifications (e.g., Kelloway et al.). Although union commitment is described as having more than one facet (e.g., union loyalty, willingness to work for the union, responsibility to the union), each appears to be fairly affective in nature. It is possible, however, that union members also develop other sorts of psychological ties to the union, such as those based on perceived costs or internalized feelings of obligation.

If this were the case, we would expect the development of continuance and normative commitment to the union to occur through the same general processes we described for commitment to the organization. It is clear, for example, that relinquishing membership in a union could have significant costs (e.g., reduced job security, restriction of employment opportunities). To the extent that union members recognized these and/or other potential costs as reasons for retaining union membership, we would expect them to develop continuance commitment to the union. Similarly, one can imagine psychological attachment to the union, based on internalized feelings about what one ought to do. These feelings could develop on the basis of union socialization practices to which new members are exposed (e.g., Fullagar, Gallagher, Gordon, & Clark, 1995) or on the basis of experiences they have early in life. Barling, Kelloway, and their colleagues have shown, for example, that affective attitudes toward unions are related to individuals' beliefs about the union attitudes their parents held (Barling, Kelloway, & Bremermann, 1991; Kelloway, Barling, & Agar, in press; Kelloway & Watts, 1994). Possibly, early family socialization experiences (including growing up in a "union family") might also influence normative commitment to the union. Finally, events may make particularly salient to union members that they are indebted to their union.

With respect to the consequences of union commitment, it is possible that continuance and normative commitment would enhance the prediction of particular union-related behaviors over that explained by affective attachment. For example, the member whose primary tie to the union is based on perceived costs would be expected to maintain membership in the union but might resist involvement in union activities, particularly those activities that did not appear to have an immediate personal benefit. Similarly, as we suggested earlier in the context of organizational commitment, it is possible that normative commitment to the union could have implications for the amount and "tone" of the effort that members will direct toward their union.

At this point, of course, all these suggestions must be considered highly speculative. Although it appears that the three-component model might generalize to occupational commitment, any conclusions about whether it also applies to union commitment or can enhance our understanding of its development or consequences await empirical research. Similarly, further research is needed before the model can be applied to other domains.

Multiple Commitments at Work

We turn our attention now to the second issue to be addressed in this chapter: that of multiple commitments at work. In describing the work done from a multiple-commitments perspective, we focus, at least initially, on affective commitment. In part, this is for the sake of simplicity. More important, however, it allows us to describe with greater accuracy the relevant multiple-commitment literature, which with few exceptions (Becker, 1992; Becker & Billings, 1993) has taken a single-component (affective) approach to the commitment construct.

Overview of the Multiple-Commitment Literature

The issue of multiple commitments has been approached by researchers in various ways. As indicated in Chapter 2, a major contribution to this literature was made by Reichers (1985), who explicitly drew together the traditional organizational-commitment literature, with its rather singular and abstract view of the organization, and the notion from organizational theory that many constituencies make up that organization.

Recognition of the existence of multiple commitments within the organization is also given in theoretical work by Lawler (1992), who reminds us that various social structures, including work organizations, place people in "multiple, nested collectivities in which they are simultaneously members of at least two groups, one encompassed within the other" (p. 327). Although Lawler was primarily interested in the influence of choice and control on affective attachment to groups, we acknowledge his work here because it represents one of the few discussions that grapple explicitly with the development of multiple commitments.

Other researchers have extended the multiple-commitment notion "outward"—that is, to domains outside the employing organization. Much of this research has focused on either the relations between organizational commitment and union commitment (e.g., Fukami & Larson, 1984; Gordon & Ladd, 1990) or the relations between organizational commitment and commitment to the profession or occupation (e.g., Aranya & Ferris, 1983; Wallace, 1993). Central to research examining links between these two pairs of commitments (organization/union, organization/occupation) is the question of compatibility, an issue we address in more detail later.

Still other researchers have examined the similarities and differences among the antecedents of commitment to various entities. Zaccaro and Dobbins (1989), for example, compared the antecedents of commitment to the organization and commitment to the work group. Barling, Fullagar, and colleagues compared the antecedents of union commitment and organizational commitment (e.g., Barling, Wade, & Fullagar, 1990; Fullagar & Barling, 1991). In both sets of research, it was concluded that commitment to the domains in question develops on the basis of their "own" unique predictors.

Perhaps most critical to an appreciation of the multiple-commitment approach is the extent to which it has "added value"; that is, if the recognition that we live in a multiple-commitment world is to have either theoretical or practical importance, it must be shown that examining commitment to various constituencies and domains refines our understanding of work-related behavior. In Chapter 2, we described research in which this was demonstrated with constituencies that are internal to the organization (Becker, 1992; Becker & Billings, 1993; Becker et al., 1996). Becker (1992), for example, showed that extra-role behavior could be best explained by considering commitment to the organization and to constituencies within it.

The value of taking a multiple-commitment approach has also been demonstrated in research that considers domains that go beyond the organization. As mentioned earlier, Meyer et al. (1993) found that the occupational commitment of nurses helped in explaining the variance in some outcome variables (e.g., intention to leave the occupation, voluntary absence) over and above that explained by organizational commitment. Moreover, affective commitment to the occupation, but not to the organization, was related to the amount of professional activity in which the nurses engaged (e.g., professional reading, attendance at conferences). In a study of professional engineers, Baugh and Roberts (1994) reported a marginally significant interaction between organizational commitment and professional commitment in the prediction of overall job performance. In their sample, the highest performers were those engineers who had strong commitment to both the organization and the engineering profession, and the lowest performers were those with weak organizational commitment and strong professional commitment.

The value of a multiple-commitment approach was also demonstrated in a study conducted by Cohen (1993b) with a sample of white-collar employees from three organizations. Cohen measured commitment to the organization, occupation, union, and job. He hypothesized that the behavior of relevance to a particular domain would be predicted best by commitment to that domain. Cohen's findings provide some support for this hypothesis. For example, the best predictor of intention to leave the organization was organizational commitment, whereas job commitment was the best predictor of job withdrawal, and union commitment was the best predictor of perceived union success. Interestingly, however, some evidence also suggested that commitments other than those to the most relevant domain enhanced the prediction of outcome measures. For example, commitment to the occupation was positively related to employees' intention to leave the job and organization; that is, those who were highly committed to their occupations indicated they were more likely to leave their current organizations and jobs than did those who were less committed. Cohen also reported that commitment to the job was positively related to union activity and that organizational commitment was negatively related to employee perceptions of union success. These findings suggest that the relations among various multiple commitments are quite complex and that both compatibility and conflict are to be expected. We turn now to a discussion of the compatibility/conflict issue.

Compatibility and Conflict

The possibility that commitments will come into conflict should not be surprising. Indeed, it would be quite naive to imagine that the goals and values of the various entities to which people can become committed will always be compatible and that the demands these make will never clash. Commitments between some pairs of domains have been expected to be less compatible than others. Questions have been raised, for example, about the inherent compatibility of organizational commitment and union commitment (e.g., Walker & Lawler, 1979). It has also been argued that members of traditional professions (e.g., lawyers, engineers) who are employed by organizations made up mainly of nonprofessionals will experience a great deal of conflict between their commitment to the profession and their commitment to the organization (Blau & Scott, 1962). Gunz and Gunz (1994, p. 802) noted that "the issue is sometimes described as zero-sum game. One can be loyal to one's profession or to one's organization, but not to both."

This zero-sum view leads to the prediction that organizational commitment might be negatively correlated with both professional and union commitment. Interestingly, however, few studies support this prediction. In a meta-analysis, Wallace (1993) reported that professional and organizational commitment were positively related. Similarly, most studies report positive correlations between commitment to the union and commitment to the organization (for a summary, see Gordon & Ladd, 1990). Thus, on the basis of this evidence, it seems quite possible for employees to feel committed to both or neither of these potentially "incompatible" domains.

The fact that commitment to these pairs of domains is not a zero-sum game does not mean, of course, that conflicts between these domains (or between constituencies within a domain) never occur or that people with multiple commitments never get "caught in the middle." Several researchers have described, for example, the conflict between commitment to the union and commitment to the organization that is felt by union stewards (e.g., Bluen & Barling, 1988; Martin & Berthiaume, 1993). Similarly, it has been suggested that organizational and professional values will not always coincide (Raelin, 1989). Committed members of work groups, departments, or divisions have also been known to disagree with the organization, to which they also feel strong commitment, about what is the "best" course of action. Finally, one can imagine situations in which an employee's commitment to a particular coworker may come into conflict with that felt toward the work group, profession, or organization.

As Reichers (1985) suggested, conflicts between entities to which people feel strong commitment are particularly painful because their commitments help shape their personal identity. Conflicts between commitments, therefore, call into question this identity. To our knowledge, no comprehensive description of conflicts between work-related commitments appears in the literature. Thus, we can only speculate about how individuals react to these painful situations.

One possibility is that individuals react to conflicts between multiple commitments by changing the intensity of the affective attachment they feel to one of the entities in question. The basis on which individuals "choose sides" is unclear, although the simplest prediction would be that people retain their affective commitment to the entity about which they felt most strongly prior to the conflict. Another possibility is that the people will reduce their commitment to the entity they consider most responsible for creating the conflict. Thus, attributional processes might play an important role.

It is also possible that frequent and/or serious conflicts will reduce the level of affective commitment to both entities, perhaps to the point that the person will want to leave one (or both). Whether voluntary turnover occurs, of course, will then depend on the extent to which employees feel bound by other psychological ties (e.g., continuance or normative commitment to one or both entities) or on whether one or both of the entities is nested in another more valued domain (e.g., an employee might want to leave the work group but be unwilling to leave the organization in order to do so).

Finally, Reichers (1985) suggested that, in extreme situations, the discomfort associated with an incompatibility between multiple commitments might be so intense that, to alleviate it, the person will choose to leave the situation altogether. In this instance, leaving is not evidence of weak commitment to any constituency (as we would typically assume), but the opposite. As with the disaffected employees described above, employees in these extreme situations might have to stay because commitment to other constituencies—and in other forms (e.g., continuance commitment)—tie them to the situation.

We can only speculate, as well, about the distribution, frequency, and intensity of the conflicts that people experience between their multiple commitments at work. That many people do develop and sustain strong multiple commitments suggests something about the nature of the conflicts. First, although some conflicts will arise unpredictably, it seems likely that many will occur in "bunches" and in conjunction with particular planned activities carried out by the various constituencies and domains (e.g., the negotiation of a collective agreement, submission of departmental budgets). If the latter is the case, it is possible that individuals will be able to reduce some of their psychological discomfort by mentally preparing for it and by focusing on the specific roles they must take on during these periods (e.g., negotiation team member, budget director). Second, it might be that conflicts between multiple commitments are relatively infrequent, occurring only occasionally throughout the person's career with a particular organization. Some of these might have intense effects on the person's emotional state for a particular period of time but have no permanent impact on the affective attachment that he or she feels to either constituency/domain. Other conflicts, however, might be quite intense and have more serious impact on the commitment to one or more of the constituencies involved.

Clearly, we need to learn much more about the conflicts among multiple commitments that people face in the workplace. Scant research has examined the nature and extent of these conflicts or how people handle them. In part, this paucity might be because of the difficulties associated with collecting relevant data about conflict experiences, particularly those with unpredictable timing. If our analysis is correct, these experiences will be relatively infrequent and idiosyncratic and might ebb and flow in a way that makes them somewhat difficult to pin down—at least by using the methods typically used by organizational researchers (surveys, questionnaires). What might be needed, to develop a more comprehensive understanding of the conflicts among multiple commitments and how people handle them, are studies into which are built the opportunity for more long-term and context-rich investigation.

At the same time, practitioners need to give some thought to how best to handle situations in which commitments come into serious conflict. Indeed, a potential downside of feeling strong affective commitment to more than one entity within the workplace is that people will find particularly painful those situations in which the entities in question make competing demands—much more so, for example, than will people with only weak affective commitment or those with strong "partisan" commitment to only one entity. Although managers within a particular domain (e.g., the organization, the union, the occupation) might not be able to intervene meaningfully in conflicts that cross domain boundaries (e.g., a conflict between the organization and the occupation), they probably can provide some assistance in dealing with conflict that occurs between constituencies within their own domain. It has been suggested, for example, that an important task for leaders of work groups is to help employees put into perspective any conflicts that occur between the work group and the larger organization. Strategies could include emphasizing the inevitability of conflict within organizational life, providing the group with sufficient background information, and developing group-level and individual-level strategies for coping with stress (Allen, 1996).

Dependencies Among Commitments

In Chapter 2, we presented a two-dimensional commitment matrix in which the three components of commitment were arrayed along one axis and various work-related entities to which one could become committed along the other (see Figure 2.1). The important implication here is that an employee's work commitment "profile" can be described in terms of the degree of affective, continuance, and normative commitment that he or she feels to each of several entities. We noted also that the matrix should not be interpreted as suggesting that each of its cells is independent. The reason is that some constituencies to which a person might belong will be nested in larger domains; thus, the person's membership with respect to one will be dependent on continued membership in the other (Lawler, 1992). Thus far, scant empirical attention has been paid to the role the nested nature of constituencies can play in helping us understand multiple commitments. Moreover, the research that has been conducted focused exclusively on affective commitment (Yoon, Baker, & Ko, 1994). Nonetheless, thinking about constituencies as being nested raises several questions about the "dependencies" that might exist among a person's multiple-workplace commitments. For the purpose of this necessarily speculative discussion, the example of a work group nested in an organization is used. It should be noted, however, that other types of dependencies exist. For example, for someone living in a small community, commitment to a profession might mean there is only one suitable employer for the person.

First, it seems reasonable to suggest that the dependencies created by nesting might influence the kind of "commitment profile" a person develops. Consider, for example, an employee with very strong affective commitment to the work group. It is possible that this individual's recognition that his or her continued membership in the group is dependent on remaining with the organization will increase the continuance commitment felt toward the organization. To do what he or she wants to do (stay in the work group), this person is required to stay in the organization. As another example, consider an employee with very strong continuance commitment to the organization. If this person also feels little affective commitment to the organization, he or she may feel somewhat "trapped" by the organization. To the extent that the employee finds this aversive, it might spill over to other constituencies nested within the organization, influencing, for example, the level of affective commitment felt to the work group or supervisor.

Second, it is possible that dependencies between multiple commitments will have an influence on the pattern of work behaviors an employee exhibits. Earlier, we noted that if our goal is to predict a behavior associated with a particular constituency, we will be most successful in doing so by using commitment to that constituency (Becker & Billings, 1993; Cohen, 1993b). For example, behavior that will benefit an employee's supervisor will be better predicted by commitment to the supervisor than by commitment to the work group. In most situations, it seems likely that this general prediction would be supported. In some situations, however, the dependencies that exist between multiple commitments might add a subtle twist to the prediction. The reason is that, because of nesting, many behaviors will appear to benefit both entities equally. In such situations, it is fairly clear what the people with commensurate (or matching) commitment will be most likely to do. If they feel strong affective commitment to both, it is likely that they will engage in the beneficial behavior; if they feel weak commitment to both, it is likely that they will not. But consider, for example, employees who feel strong affective commitment to their organization but weak affective commitment to their work group. These employees might be motivated to help the organization but not the work group; the dilemma, of course, is that by not helping the work group, they also fail to help the organization. In such situations, it might be that constituency-focused commitment will be less predictive of behavior than other factors. A better predictor might be the kind of explanation the employee is given (either directly or by cues in the environment) for a particular behavioral direction. For example, a senior manager might make particularly salient to the employee the value of the behavior for the organization. This sort of cue, then, allows the employee to account for his or her behavior in a satisfactory way ("This isn't for my work group; I am doing it for the good of my organization").

Summary

In this chapter, we examined the extension of the three-component model to domains other than the organization. Research findings suggest that individuals experience affective, continuance, and normative commitment to their occupations and that these can contribute beyond organizational commitment to our understanding of particular work behaviors. Although it is possible that these components of commitment are also applicable to other domains and to constituencies within these domains, this possibility awaits further research.

We also considered the relations between the various work-related entities to which people become committed, speculating on the nature of the conflicts and dependencies between these commitments. In this regard, we end where we began, with the reminder that commitment within the workplace involves both multiple forms and multiple foci. Although this approach is clearly more complex, it promises to enhance significantly what we know about the development and consequences of and changes in commitment—in all senses of the word. It may also assist us in making sense, and in helping others make sense, of the various entities to which they are psychologically attached.

A Look Back
and a Look Ahead

A s has no doubt become apparent, many factors are involved in the commitment process. Our objective of this chapter is to provide an overview of what we know and what we have yet to learn about this process. Figure 7.1 provides a summary of the key variables involved and their relations and serves as a guide for this review. We begin by looking back at the research to determine what we have learned and how this knowledge can be applied. This look back also identifies gaps in our understanding. We conclude by looking ahead at the research that needs to be done to fill these gaps.

A Look Back

To begin our look back, consider the nature of the commitment construct itself. The general consensus now is that organizational commitment is a multidimen-

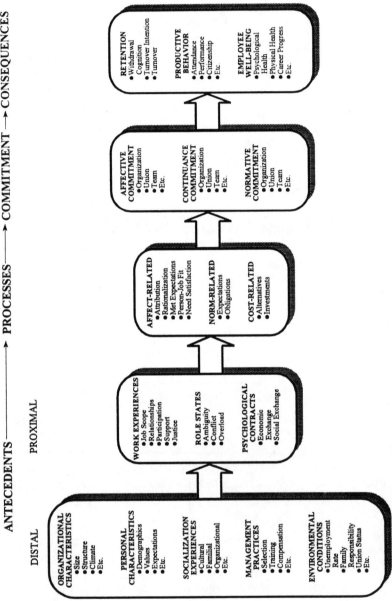

Figure 7.1. A multidimensional model of organizational commitment, its antecedents, and its consequences

sional construct. Commitment can take different forms and can be directed at different constituencies within the organization. The importance of distinguishing among these different forms and foci of commitments is illustrated by the evidence that they relate somewhat differently to behavior. Despite the recognition of its multidimensionality, clearly an imbalance exists in the attention that has been given to the different forms and foci. Most widely studied has been affective commitment to the organization as a whole. In part, this emphasis reflects the fact that recognition of the multidimensional nature of organizational commitment is relatively recent. Evidence obtained since these distinctions have been made, however, continues to suggest that affective commitment to the organization has the strongest and most consistent relations with desirable outcomes (e.g., retention, attendance, performance, citizenship). This suggestion could be interpreted to mean that we need only consider affective commitment to the organization in the future. We have suggested, at various points throughout this book, why this tactic would not be advisable. We offer a few more reasons here.

First, by failing to recognize that commitment can take different forms, we run the risk of assuming that if (affective) commitment leads to retention, an employee who remains must be affectively committed. Alternatively, we might assume that if we can get an employee to stay, he or she will become affectively committed. The former assumption need not be true; the latter can have disappointing consequences. For example, organizations that attempt to get employees committed by making the cost of leaving prohibitive run the risk of creating continuance commitment, which, as you saw in Chapter 3, does not have the same positive implications for on-the-job behavior and performance that affective commitment does. Indeed, it can have exactly the opposite effects. Similarly, using a paternalistic approach to management in an attempt to get employees committed can lead to a greater sense of obligation than desire to remain. Although the evidence suggests that normative commitment also relates positively to desirable forms of organizational behavior, the relations are typically not as strong. Moreover, it has been suggested that the effects of normative commitment might not be as long-lasting or pervasive as those of affective commitment (see Meyer & Allen, 1991).

Second, concluding on the basis of existing evidence that affective commitment is the most desirable form of commitment and the only form that really matters could be considered ethnocentric (cf. Boyacigiller & Adler, 1991; Hofstede, 1980; Randall, 1993). Although affective commitment has been found to have the strongest links with desirable outcomes in North America, where the vast majority of the research has been done, it is possible that other forms of commitment play a greater role in other cultures. Normative commitment, for example, might be a better predictor than affective commitment in collectivist cultures that emphasize strong social ties (and obligations) and in cultures characterized by uncertainty avoidance where loyalty is considered a virtue (see Hofstede for a more detailed discussion of the conceptualization and measurement of cultural differences). This prospect could explain why investigators who compared the (affective) commitment of Japanese and American workers have been surprised to find that American workers are *more* committed than their Japanese counterparts (e.g., Lincoln, 1989; Luthans, McCaul, & Dodd, 1985; Near, 1989). Japanese culture is more collectivist and uncertainty avoidant than is U.S. culture. There is reason to suspect, therefore, that if normative commitment had been measured instead of affective commitment, the findings might have been different. Indeed, in her summary of the results of a case study conducted by Rohlen (1974), Near (p. 295) noted,

> Japanese workers were found to avoid quitting their jobs even when they desired to do so. The lack of available job opportunities and the normative pressures expressed by their co-workers and friends seemed to be sufficient to persuade them to stay, in most cases.

Finally, distinguishing among different forms of commitment helps in defining the boundaries of the construct. Before efforts were made to distinguish different components of commitment, definitions of the construct were quite loose and permitted considerable latitude in the development of measures and the generation of hypotheses. When viewed as a unidimensional construct, most definitions of commitment placed a strong emphasis on affective attachment but also included varying degrees of cost perception and moral obligation. This was true also of the measures that were developed. Once the distinctions are made, construct definitions become tighter, and it is easier to develop and evaluate the psychometric properties of measures.

Distinguishing among the constituencies to which employees become committed is also potentially important, although the research is limited. In Chapter 2, we discussed some evidence suggesting the value of distinguishing among constituencies within the organization; that is, behavior might be best predicted from commitment to the constituency for which the behavior has the greatest impact. In Chapter 6, we noted that commitments to domains other than the organization (e.g., occupation, profession, union) can have an influence on organization-relevant behavior, as well as on behavior of relevance to that domain. Research concerning compatibility and conflict among multiple commitments is still in its infancy but is sure to develop in the future.

Turning to the left side of Figure 7.1, we see that many factors are implicated in the development of commitment. We make distinctions here, as we have in previous chapters, between proximal and distal causes of commitment. Among the more proximal causes are employees' work experiences, their role states, and the psychological contract defining their exchange relationship with the organization. The more distal causes include organizational characteristics, personal characteristics of the employee, preentry socialization experiences, management practices, and environmental conditions. These distal causes exert their influence on commitment through their influence on the more proximal causes (cf. Mathieu, 1988; Mathieu & Hamel, 1989). For example, characteristics of an organization, such as its size, are unlikely to influence commitment directly; rather, they affect commitment because of the effect they have on employees' experiences (e.g., ability to participate in decision making) and role states. As we noted in Chapter 5 and as indicated in Figure 7.1, organizational management practices are best considered distal causes of commitment. We discuss the implications of this below.

In the middle of Figure 7.1 are what we referred to in Chapter 4 as *process variables.* These are the mechanisms through which the antecedent variables are presumed to operate. We really know relatively little at this point about many of these mechanisms. Some of those that we have included in the figure as processes operating in the development of affective commitment (e.g., need satisfaction) have long been assumed to operate but have not or cannot be studied empirically. Others (e.g., person-job fit, met expectations) have been studied, but for various reasons (e.g., use of inappropriate methods) the findings are difficult to interpret. Still others have yet to receive adequate attention (e.g., attribution). Although we describe these here and elsewhere as process variables, some might argue that they are simply mediators (even more proximal causes) or moderators (necessary conditions for effects) of what we listed as proximal antecedents. We would not argue with this. What is important to recognize is that these variables play an important role in helping us understand the reasons why other variables are correlated with commitment. As will be seen below, they also help us go beyond existing findings to speculate on how organizational actions might affect employees' commitment. We know even less about the mechanisms involved in the development of normative and continuance commitment than we do about those implicated in the development of affective commitment. We can only speculate that environmental conditions must in some way stimulate employees to believe that they have an obligation to the organization or that it would be costly to leave.

Returning to the issue of management practices, we noted in Chapter 5 that these are best considered distal causes of commitment. From a practical standpoint, recognizing this point creates an awareness that *doing* something might not be enough. Employees will have to perceive that it was done, attribute the action to the organization, and interpret it as being motivated by good intentions. One cannot assume that these perceptions will take place automatically. To the contrary, managerial actions can often be interpreted in more than one way, with each having somewhat different implications. To illustrate, Niehoff and Moorman (1993) examined the impact of managerial monitoring behavior on employees' organizational citizenship behavior (willingness to do little extras to help out). Their findings suggest that monitoring can have positive or negative effects on citizenship behavior, depending on how it is perceived; monitoring perceived as an attempt to control had a negative effect, whereas monitoring perceived as a means of obtaining fair and unbiased performance data had a more positive effect. Communication, therefore, is very important. Management not only should inform employees of its actions and intentions but also should listen to or seek out the reactions of employees to determine whether the message has been accurately received. Where appropriate, input from employees should also be sought before policies and practices are implemented.

On the basis of the findings reported in Chapter 5, it appears that organizations can do several things to foster a stronger sense of commitment in their employees. Providing accurate information to employees during the recruitment and selection process, using socialization strategies designed to bolster employees' sense of self-worth, and offering training programs to provide employees with the knowledge and skills they require to do their jobs effectively are just some things that organizations can do. Admittedly, however, the amount of empirical research that examines the impact of HRM and other management practices on commitment is limited. For this reason, practitioners might also want to pay attention to the more "basic" research concerning antecedents and processes involved in the development of commitment. By understanding how commitment develops, practitioners will be in a better position to anticipate the impact of a particular policy or practice even if it has not yet been the subject of empirical research. For example, little or no research examines how performance appraisals affect commitment per se. Nevertheless, knowing that employees react favorably to the outcomes of other practices when they believe the procedures used to determine them were fair should sensitize us to the fact that the same is likely to be true in the case of performance appraisal. It then becomes a matter of looking to justice theory and research to determine what factors influence perceptions of fairness and then designing an appraisal system accordingly. For instance, Leventhal (1980) identified six criteria used to evaluate the fairness of decision-making procedures: (a) consistency across time and people, (b) absence of self-interest, (c) use of accurate information, (d) opportunity for correction of errors, (e) concern for the interests of all involved, and (f) application of ethical and moral standards. It is a reasonably safe bet that performance appraisal procedures designed to meet these criteria will be more likely to contribute to the development or maintenance of affective commitment than will those that are not.

In summary, we know considerably more today about the commitment process than we did a decade or two ago. As can be seen from Figure 7.1, the process is complex. Some links among the variables involved in this process have been reasonably well established and can serve as a guide to those who are interested primarily in application. Others are based more on speculation than on evidence at this point. Moreover, some variables not included in the model should be. We turn now to a discussion of what we consider to be among the most obvious gaps in our understanding and how we might fill them.

A Look Ahead

Throughout this book, we identified issues that need to be addressed. Some are long-standing, whereas others have arisen only recently as the result of our efforts to answer other questions. Still others stem from the fact that the world of work is changing in ways that have implications for the meaning, consequences, and development of commitment. We bring together here what we consider to be some of the more pressing issues.

Meaning of Commitment

More attention has been given to distinguishing among different forms, or components, of commitment than to distinguishing among the foci (targets) of commitment, both within and outside the organization. Nevertheless, more work is needed in both areas. As we noted in Chapter 2, the consensus concerning the multidimensional nature of commitment is not accompanied by agreement with regard to the different forms commitment can take. Some confusion is created by the existence of different frameworks and the use of different terms to mean the same thing and the same terms to mean different things. Although we are not advocating that other interesting questions be put on hold until a consensus can be reached, we do caution that progress in these other areas will be hindered unless researchers are clear about what forms of commitment they are examining and ensure that the measures they use have demonstrated construct validity (see Schwab, 1980).

Recognizing that multiple foci of commitment exist raises several interesting questions: What defines the boundaries for the various foci? What determines to which foci an employee becomes committed? Under what conditions are commitments to these different foci likely to be compatible or to conflict? How do these multiple commitments combine to shape employees' behavior? Some of the research we reviewed in Chapters 2 and 6 starts to address these questions, but much more work is necessary.

Finally, we need to determine whether the "meaning" of commitment is the same in other cultures. Although some research we reviewed in this book was conducted outside North America, much of that was conducted in English-speaking countries in the Western world. Relatively few studies were conducted elsewhere in the world; even fewer involved the collection of data in more than one country or culture. What is needed is systematic investigation of the dimensionality of commitment across cultures. Once it can be determined whether the multidimensional conceptualizations developed in North America apply in other cultures, additional cross-cultural research can be conducted to assess the generalizability of findings concerning the development and consequences of commitment. The results of such research might be of particular interest to multinational organizations interested in maintaining a committed workforce in their worldwide operations.

Consequences of Commitment

The most widely studied consequence of commitment has been employee retention. More attention has been paid recently to other outcomes, such as absenteeism, job performance, and citizenship behavior, but there is still a need to examine how these outcomes are related to different forms of commitment and to commitment to different foci or constituencies. More attention also needs to be paid to potential negative consequences of commitment (see Randall, 1987). Are committed employees more likely to blindly accept the status quo even if it is not in the long-term interest of the employee or the organization? Are committed employees more likely to voice their concerns if they believe it is in the organization's best interests to do so? Are committed employees more likely to behave unethically if they view such behavior as being of service to the organization? Does the likelihood of engaging in these behaviors vary as a function of the nature or focus of the commitment?

As we noted in Chapter 3, investigation of the consequences of commitment has focused primarily on outcomes of relevance to the organization. Although we see some indication that commitment might also have benefits for the employee, too little research has been conducted on which to draw firm conclusions. It is likely that the benefits of being committed will vary with the nature of the commitment, but this, too, is only speculation at this point.

One concern that has often been raised about consequence research is that research designs are not adequate to determine cause and effect. Although it is not feasible to use experimental methods to examine the impact of organizational commitment as an independent variable, the use of causal modeling procedures in future research will permit greater confidence in causal inference than simple correlations. Ideally, such research should be conducted by using longitudinal designs with time lags appropriate to the variables involved. In cases where it is difficult to determine what the appropriate time lag might be, obtaining measures on repeated occasions can be informative (see Griffin, 1991, for an example). Care should also be taken to ensure that the appropriate level of analysis is used. Most research has been conducted at an individual level of analysis (relating the commitment of individuals to their behavior). Indeed, this approach is appropriate for addressing some research questions. It is arguably also an easier approach to use. Nevertheless, organization-level analyses are more appropriate for addressing other questions, and as you saw in Chapter 3, studies using this approach, albeit limited, have provided some interesting results (e.g., Angle & Perry, 1981; Ostroff, 1992).

Development of Commitment

Figure 7.1 does not do justice to the wide array of variables that have been found over the years to correlate with commitment. We see little need for more research to examine bivariate correlations. There is a need, however, for more research to examine the causal ordering of variables in the development process, as well as to identify conditions that might moderate the relations between antecedent variables and commitment. To make a substantial contribution to our understanding of the development of commitment, however, such research should have a solid grounding in theory. Moreover, where possible, experimental and quasi-experimental studies should be conducted to establish causal connections.

Where it is necessary to rely on causal modeling procedures, the same cautions mentioned in the discussion of consequences apply.

Of perhaps most obvious interest to the practitioner will be research conducted to examine how what practitioners do affects the commitment of the employees in the organizations for which the practitioners work. We noted in Chapter 5 that research has only recently been undertaken to examine the influence of HRM practices on commitment. The research findings suggest that these practices can have an effect, but the data are limited. As Huselid (1995) pointed out, it is difficult to interpret the results of studies that address only one practice at a time. More research is needed to examine the impact of entire HRM systems. Where interest is in a particular practice, it is important to measure and control for other components in the system.

Finally, much more attention needs to be given to process issues than has been the case to this point. As we noted above, understanding *why* commitment develops is as important from a practical perspective as it is from an academic one. Kanter (1983) illustrated this point nicely with reference to an ancient parable: Wisdom has it that the Chinese first discovered the benefits of cooking meat when a pig was accidentally incinerated in a house fire. Fortunately, cooks of the future recognized heat as the mediating mechanism and did not feel compelled to torch a house in order to prepare dinner. As we can gain better insight into the mechanisms involved in the formation of commitment, we will be in a better position to design HRM systems that can be applied to develop desired levels of commitment effectively and efficiently without producing undesirable side effects.

Commitment in the Changing World of Work

Perhaps the biggest challenge for commitment researchers will be to determine how commitment is affected by the many changes (e.g., increased global competition, reengineering, downsizing) that are occurring in the world of work (see Cascio, 1995). We noted in Chapter 1 that, unlike those who say these changes make organizational commitment an outdated construct, we believe commitment will be as important or even more important in the future than it was in the past (cf. Reichheld, 1996). Admittedly, organizations are likely to employ fewer people, but the employees they retain will be asked to do more and to take more responsibility. Organizations are also likely to invest a great deal in these employees (e.g., through training) and to be in competition with other organizations for their services. Similarly, organizations will want to ensure that those who provide services on a contract basis will be committed to fulfilling their contracts. And finally, if, as recent research suggests, commitment has benefits to individuals as well as to organizations, they will be seeking a foci for their commitment.

We have learned a great deal about commitment by studying it in the context of commitment to organizations. This knowledge will likely be applicable to organizations for some time to come. Moreover, it should serve as a guide in the study of other work-related commitments, including those that we have already begun to study (e.g., occupation, profession, union), as well as others that we have yet to envision.

Appendix

Measurement of Affective, Continuance, and Normative Commitment

A s we noted in Chapter 2, it is now generally recognized that commitment is a multidimensional construct. Our own research in the area of organizational commitment began with an attempt to illustrate how inconsistencies in the conceptualization and measurement of commitment might interfere with our understanding of the commitment process (Meyer & Allen, 1984). This early work led ultimately to the development of a three-component model of commitment and of measures of the three components: affective, continuance, and normative commitment (Allen & Meyer, 1990a; Meyer & Allen, 1991). This three-component framework served as the basis for our subsequent research and, in large measure, provides the structure for our discussion of commitment throughout this book.

Although of seemingly less relevance than research conducted to examine the development and consequences of commitment, particularly to those with applied interests, research conducted for purposes of development and evaluation of commitment measures is nevertheless important. Indeed, the meaningfulness of substantive research depends on it. In this appendix, we present the Affective, Continuance, and Normative Commitment Scales referred to throughout this book, briefly describe how they were developed, and summarize the results of recent research as they pertain to the psychometric properties of these measures. A more complete review of this research is provided by Allen and Meyer (1996).

Schwab (1980) outlined a set of recommendations for the psychometric evaluation of measures used in organizational behavior research. Included among the recommendations is an examination of the reliability (e.g., internal consistency, temporal stability) and factor structure of the measures. Items within a scale should measure the same construct, scale scores should be relatively stable across time (assuming no major changes in conditions that influence the construct), and items written to measure one construct should not correlate highly with items intended to measure unrelated constructs. Beyond this, Schwab noted that the construct validity of a measure can be assessed by examining its correlations with other constructs and comparing these correlations with what is expected theoretically. In the case of the Affective, Continuance, and Normative Commitment Scales being evaluated here, the three-component model described by Meyer and Allen (1991) provides such a theoretical framework, or "nomological net" (Cronbach & Meehl, 1955).

Development of the Measures

Development of the Affective, Continuance, and Normative Commitment Scales was based on the scale construction principles outlined by Jackson (1970) and described in detail elsewhere (Allen & Meyer, 1990a). Briefly, definitions of the three constructs were used to develop an initial pool of items that was then administered to a sample of men and women working in various occupations and organizations. Items were selected for inclusion in the scales on the basis of a series of decision rules that took into account the distribution of responses on the 7-point agree-disagree scale for each item, item-scale correlations, content redundancy, and the desire to include both positively and negatively keyed items. Each of the three scales resulting from this process comprised 8 items. These items are presented in Table A.1.

TABLE A.1 Affective, Continuance, and Normative Commitment Scales

Affective Commitment Scale Items

1. I would be very happy to spend the rest of my career in this organization.

2. I enjoy discussing my organization with people outside it.[a]

3. I really feel as if this organization's problems are my own.

4. I think I could easily become as attached to another organization as I am to this one. (R)[a]

5. I do not feel like "part of the family" at my organization. (R)

6. I do not feel "emotionally attached" to this organization. (R)

7. This organization has a great deal of personal meaning for me.

8. I do not feel a strong sense of belonging to my organization. (R)

Continuance Commitment Scale Items

1. I am not afraid of what might happen if I quit my job without having another one lined up. (R)[a]

2. It would be very hard for me to leave my organization right now, even if I wanted to.

3. Too much of my life would be disrupted if I decided I wanted to leave my organization right now.

4. It wouldn't be too costly for me to leave my organization in the near future. (R)[a]

5. Right now, staying with my organization is a matter of necessity as much as desire.

6. I believe that I have too few options to consider leaving this organization.

7. One of the few negative consequences of leaving this organization would be the scarcity of available alternatives.

8. One of the major reasons I continue to work for this organization is that leaving would require considerable personal sacrifice; another organization may not match the overall benefits I have here.

9. If I had not already put so much of myself into this organization, I might consider working elsewhere.[b]

A revision of the three scales was undertaken recently in response to some of the findings reported below. The revision was most extensive in the case of normative commitment (see Meyer et al., 1993). The revised scales are also

TABLE A.1 Continued

Normative Commitment Scale Items (Original)

1. I think that people these days move from company to company too often.

2. I do not believe that a person must always be loyal to his or her organization. (R)

3. Jumping from organization to organization does not seem at all unethical to me. (R)

4. One of the major reasons I continue to work for this organization is that I believe loyalty is important and therefore feel a sense of moral obligation to remain.

5. If I got another offer for a better job elsewhere, I would not feel it was right to leave my organization.

6. I was taught to believe in the value of remaining loyal to one organization.

7. Things were better in the days when people stayed with one organization for most of their careers.

8. I do not think that wanting to be a "company man" or "company woman" is sensible anymore. (R)

Normative Commitment Scale Items (Revised)

1. I do not feel any obligation to remain with my current employer. (R)

2. Even if it were to my advantage, I do not feel it would be right to leave my organization now.

3. I would feel guilty if I left my organization now.

4. This organization deserves my loyalty.

5. I would not leave my organization right now because I have a sense of obligation to the people in it.

6. I owe a great deal to my organization.

NOTE: Responses to each item are made on a 7-point scale with anchors labeled (1) *strongly disagree* and (7) *strongly agree*. R indicates a reverse-keyed item (scoring is reversed). The original scales comprise 8 items each (Allen & Meyer, 1990a); the revised scales each comprise 6 items (Meyer et al., 1993). For administration, items from the three scales are mixed to form a 24- (original) or 18- (revised) item series.
a Item included in the original but not in the revised scales.
b Item included in the revised Continuance Commitment Scale only.

reported in Table A.1. In the review that follows, no distinction is made between the original and revised scales except where analyses addressed the revision specifically.

Reliability Estimates

Internal Consistency

Internal consistency of the three scales has typically been estimated by using coefficient alpha. The number of estimates obtained for the three scales range from a low of 20 for the Normative Commitment Scale to a high of more than 40 for the Affective Commitment Scale. Median reliabilities for the Affective, Continuance, and Normative Commitment Scales, respectively, are .85, .79, and .73 (for actual estimates across studies, see Allen & Meyer, 1996, Table 1). With few exceptions, reliability estimates exceed .70.

Temporal Stability

Temporal stability is evaluated by correlating measures of commitment obtained at different times (test-retest reliability). Relatively few published studies have reported test-retest reliability estimates, and those that have, have typically collected data from newcomers at various points during their first year of employment. Temporal stability tends to be lower when commitment is measured very early in employees' careers. Vandenberg and Self (1993), for example, found test-retest reliabilities as low as .38 for affective commitment and .44 for continuance commitment when commitment measured on the first day of work was correlated with commitment 6 months later. Meyer et al. (1991) and Meyer et al. (1993) found reliability estimates above .60 when the measures of affective, continuance, and normative commitment included in the correlation were obtained after at least 1 month on the job. Blau, Paul, and St. John (1993) found a test-retest reliability coefficient of .94 for the Affective Commitment Scale when administered 7 weeks apart to a sample of employees with an average tenure of more than 5 years. Together, these findings suggest that, as might be expected, commitment is in a state of flux in the early period of employment but quickly begins to stabilize.

Factor Structure

The factor structure of the commitment measures has been examined in several studies using both exploratory and confirmatory analyses. Some analyses include items from all three measures; others included only Affective Commitment Scale and/or Continuance Commitment Scale items. For the most part, the results of both the exploratory (Allen & Meyer, 1990a; McGee & Ford, 1987; Reilly & Orsak, 1991) and confirmatory (Dunham et al., 1994; Hackett et al., 1994; Meyer, Allen, & Gellatly, 1990; Moorman et al., 1993; Shore & Tetrick, 1991; Somers, 1993; Vandenberghe, 1996) studies provide evidence to suggest that affective, continuance, and normative commitment are indeed distinguishable constructs. (For a more detailed summary of results, see Allen & Meyer, 1996.)

Factor analyses have also been conducted to determine whether the commitment measures are distinguishable from related constructs. These studies have provided evidence that the three commitment constructs are indeed distinguishable from measures of job satisfaction (Shore & Tetrick, 1991), career, job, and work values (Blau et al., 1993), career commitment (Reilly & Orsak, 1991), occupational commitment (Meyer et al., 1993), and perceived organizational support (Shore & Tetrick). This evidence helps in addressing concerns raised by Morrow (1983) about the contribution made by organizational commitment research (see Chapter 2 and Morrow, 1993, for a more detailed discussion of this issue).

Tests of the Nomological Net

As noted above, the three-component model of commitment developed by Allen and Meyer (1990a; Meyer & Allen, 1991) outlines a set of hypothesized relations between the three commitment variables and other variables presumed to be antecedents and consequences of commitment. By demonstrating that the pattern of empirical findings matches the hypothesized pattern, further evidence is provided for the construct validity of the measures. We discuss the results of relevant studies (e.g., Allen & Meyer, 1990a; Bycio et al., 1995; Dunham et al., 1994; Hackett et al., 1994; Konovsky & Cropanzano, 1991; Meyer et al., 1990; Shore & Wayne, 1993; Whitener & Walz, 1993) in considerable detail in Chapters 3 and 4 and, therefore, do not do so again here. These findings are also discussed by Allen and Meyer (1996) specifically as they pertain to the construct validity of the measures. In general, the findings tend to be consistent with the prediction and add to our confidence in the construct validity of the measures.

Unresolved Issues

Despite the generally supportive evidence described above, some findings suggest the need for further refinements in the conceptualization and measurement of commitment. Most notably, the Continuance Commitment Scale has been found in some studies to comprise two related dimensions—one reflecting lack of alternatives, and the other high personal sacrifice (Hackett et al., 1994; McGee & Ford, 1987; Meyer et al., 1990; Somers, 1993). The implications of this are unclear. McGee and Ford found that the two subscales correlated in opposite directions with affective commitment and concluded that these subscales measure somewhat different constructs. They advocated further development of the subscales. In contrast, others have found that the two dimensions/subscales are highly related and correlate similarly with other constructs (e.g., Hackett et al., 1994; Meyer et al., 1989). These findings, combined with evidence that the internal consistency of the full Continuance Commitment Scale is acceptable (Allen & Meyer, 1996), suggest that little may be gained by further development of the subscales. Nevertheless, users might be wise to evaluate the utility of using subscales on a case-by-case basis until this issue is resolved (Meyer et al., 1990).

Studies have also revealed stronger than expected correlations between the Affective Commitment Scale and the Normative Commitment Scale, suggesting that feelings of affective attachment and sense of obligation to an organization are not independent of one another (e.g., Hackett et al., 1994). The two scales also tend to show similar patterns of correlations with antecedent (particularly work experience) and outcome measures; the correlations involving the Affective Commitment Scale, however, tend to be somewhat stronger than those involving the Normative Commitment Scale (see Allen & Meyer, 1996). A recent modification of the Normative Commitment Scale did not correct these problems (Meyer et al., 1993).

Finally, Vandenberg and Self (1993) found that the factor structure of the Affective Commitment Scale and the Continuance Commitment Scale was somewhat unstable during the early months of employment, and the researchers cautioned that the scales might not be appropriate for use with new employees. Meyer and Gardner (1994) conducted similar analyses, however, and found little evidence of instability. The difference in findings might be because of differences in the timing of measurement in the two studies; Vandenberg and Self obtained their measures after 1 day, 1 month, and 3 months, whereas Meyer and Gardner administered their measures after 1, 6, and 12 months. In the light of these findings, researchers wanting to use these measures to examine changes in commitment and/or its correlations with other variables over time should determine that the factor structure is indeed stable over the time frame examined.

Summary and Conclusions

The findings reported here provide considerable support for the reliability and validity of the Affective, Continuance, and Normative Commitment Scales. Construct validation is, of course, an ongoing process. We identified a few areas where further investigation is required and acknowledge that others might arise as additional research is conducted.

Space does not permit us to provide a detailed review of other measures of commitment used in the research described in this book. Of these measures, the Organizational Commitment Questionnaire has received the most thorough and generally positive evaluation (see Mowday et al., 1979, and Mowday et al., 1982, for details). The measures of identification, internalization, and compliance developed by O'Reilly and Chatman (1986) have received somewhat mixed reviews (e.g., Caldwell et al., 1990; Harris et al., 1993; O'Reilly et al., 1991; Vandenberg et al., 1994). Becker and his colleagues (Becker, 1992; Becker et al., 1996) have developed modified versions of the identification and internalization constructs that show some promise. Measures used in other studies (e.g., Jaros et al., 1993; Mayer & Schoorman, 1992; Penley & Gould, 1988) have not received enough attention to provide an adequate evaluation at this time. As we noted in Chapter 2, consumers of commitment research should be sensitive to the considerable variability in the nature and quality of measures used. Moreover, scale labels and construct definitions can sometimes be confusing.

References

Adkins, C. L. (1995). Previous work experience and organizational socialization: A longitudinal examination. *Academy of Management Journal, 38,* 839-862.

Allen, N. J. (1996). Affective reactions to the group and the organization. In M. A. West (Ed.), *Handbook of work group psychology* (pp. 371-396). Chichester, UK: Wiley.

Allen, N. J., & Meyer, J. P. (1990a). The measurement and antecedents of affective, continuance, and normative commitment to the organization. *Journal of Occupational Psychology, 63,* 1-18.

Allen, N. J., & Meyer, J. P. (1990b). Organizational socialization tactics: A longitudinal analysis of links to newcomers' commitment and role orientation. *Academy of Management Journal, 33,* 847-858.

Allen, N. J., & Meyer, J. P. (1993). Organizational commitment: Evidence of career stage effects? *Journal of Business Research, 26,* 49-61.

Allen, N. J., & Meyer, J. P. (1996). Affective, continuance, and normative commitment to the organization: An examination of construct validity. *Journal of Vocational Behavior, 49,* 252-276.

Alutto, J. A., Hrebiniak, L. G., & Alonso, R. C. (1973). On operationalizing the concept of commitment. *Social Forces, 51,* 448-454.

Angle, H. L., & Lawson, M. B. (1994). Organizational commitment and employees' performance ratings: Both type of commitment and type of performance count. *Psychological Reports, 75,* 1539-1551.

Angle, H. L., & Perry, J. L. (1981). An empirical assessment of organizational commitment and organizational effectiveness. *Administrative Science Quarterly, 27,* 1-14.

Aranya, N., & Ferris, K. R. (1983). Organizational-professional conflict among U.S. and Israeli professional accountants. *Journal of Social Psychology, 119,* 153-161.

Argyris, C. P. (1960). *Understanding organizational behavior.* Belmont, CA: Dorsey.

Arthur, J. B. (1992). The link between business strategy and industrial relations systems in American steel minimills. *Industrial and Labor Relations Review, 45,* 488-506.

Arthur, J. B. (1994). Effects of human resource systems on manufacturing performance and turnover. *Academy of Management Journal, 37,* 670-687.

Ashford, S. J., Lee, C., & Bobko, P. (1989). Content, causes, and consequences of job insecurity: A theory-based measure and substantive test. *Academy of Management Journal, 32,* 803-829.

Ashforth, B. E., & Saks, A. M. (1996). Socialization tactics: Longitudinal effects on newcomer adjustment. *Academy of Management Journal, 39,* 149-178.

Aven, F. F., Jr., Parker, B., & McEvoy, G. M. (1993). Gender and attitudinal commitment to organizations: A meta-analysis. *Journal of Business Research, 26,* 63-73.

Baker, H. E., & Feldman, D. C. (1990). Strategies of organizational socialization and their impact on newcomer adjustment. *Journal of Managerial Issues, 11,* 198-212.

Barling, J., Kelloway, E. K., & Bremermann, E. H. (1991). Pre-employment predictors of union attitudes: The role of family socialization and work beliefs. *Journal of Applied Psychology, 76,* 725-731.

Barling, J., Wade, B., & Fullagar, C. (1990). Predicting employee commitment to company and union: Divergent models. *Journal of Occupational Commitment, 63,* 49-61.

Bashaw, E. R., & Grant, S. E. (1994). Exploring the distinctive nature of work commitments: Their relationships with personal characteristics, job performance, and propensity to leave. *Journal of Personal Selling and Sales Management, 14,* 41-56.

Bateman, T. S., & Strasser, S. (1984). A longitudinal analysis of the antecedents of organizational commitment. *Academy of Management Journal, 27,* 95-112.

Baugh, S. G., & Roberts, R. M. (1994). Professional and organizational commitment among engineers: Conflicting or complementing? *IEEE Transactions on Engineering Management, 41,* 108-114.

Becker, H. S. (1960). Notes on the concept of commitment. *American Journal of Sociology, 66,* 32-42.

Becker, T. E. (1992). Foci and bases of commitment: Are they distinctions worth making? *Academy of Management Journal, 35,* 232-244.

Becker, T. E., & Billings, R. S. (1993). Profiles of commitment: An empirical test. *Journal of Organizational Behavior, 14,* 177-190.

Becker, T. E., Billings, R. S., Eveleth, D. M., & Gilbert, N. L. (1996). Foci and bases of employee commitment: Implications for job performance. *Academy of Management Journal, 39,* 464-482.

Begley, T. M., & Czajka, J. M. (1993). Panel analysis of the moderating effects of commitment on job satisfaction, intent to quit, and health following organizational change. *Journal of Applied Psychology, 78,* 552-556.

Black, J. S., Gregersen, H. B., & Mendenhall, M. E. (1992). *Global assignments.* San Francisco: Jossey-Bass.

Blau, G., & Boal, K. (1989). Using job involvement and organizational commitment interactively to predict turnover. *Journal of Management, 15,* 115-127.

Blau, G., Paul, A., & St. John, N. (1993). On developing a general index of work commitment. *Journal of Vocational Behavior, 42,* 298-314.

Blau, G. J. (1985). The measurement and prediction of career commitment. *Journal of Occupational Psychology, 58,* 277-288.

Blau, G. J. (1987). Using a person-environment fit model to predict job involvement and organizational commitment. *Journal of Vocational Behavior, 30,* 240-257.

Blau, P. M., & Scott, W. R. (1962). *Formal organization.* San Francisco: Chandler.

Blood, M. R. (1969). Work values and job satisfaction. *Journal of Applied Psychology, 53,* 456-459.

Bluen, S. D., & Barling, J. (1988). Psychological stressors associated with industrial relations. In C. L. Cooper & R. Payne (Eds.), *Causes, coping, and consequences of stress at work* (pp. 175-205). Chichester, UK: Wiley.

Boyacigiller, N., & Adler, N. J. (1991). The parochial dinosaur: Organizational science in the global context. *Academy of Management Review, 16,* 262-290.

Breaugh, J. A. (1983). Realistic job previews: A critical appraisal and future research directions. *Academy of Management Review, 8,* 612-619.

Brett, J. E., Cron, W. L., & Slocum, J. W. (1995). Economic dependency on work: A moderator of the relationship between organizational commitment and performance. *Academy of Management Journal, 38,* 261-271.

Bridges, W. (1994). *Jobshift: How to prosper in a workplace without jobs.* Reading, MA: Addison-Wesley.

Brockner, J. (1992). The escalation of commitment to a failing course of action: Toward theoretical progress. *Academy of Management Review, 17,* 39-61.

Brockner, J., DeWitt, R., Grover, S. L., & Reed, T. (1990). When it is especially important to explain why: Factors affecting the relationship between managers' explanations of a layoff and survivors' reaction to the layoff. *Journal of Experimental Social Psychology, 26,* 389-407.

Brockner, J., Grover, S., Reed, T., DeWitt, R., & O'Malley, M. (1987). Survivors' reactions to layoffs: We get by with a little help from our friends. *Administrative Science Quarterly, 32,* 526-542.

Brockner, J., Tyler, T. R., & Cooper-Schneider, R. (1992). The influence of prior commitment to an institution on reactions to perceived unfairness: The higher they are, the harder they fall. *Administrative Science Quarterly, 37,* 241-261.

Brockner, J., Weisenfeld, B. M., Reed, T., Grover, S., & Martin, C. (1993). Interactive effect of job content and content on the reactions of layoff survivors. *Journal of Personality and Social Psychology, 64,* 187-197.

Brooke, P. P., Russell, D. W., & Price, J. L. (1988). Discriminant validation of measures of job satisfaction, job involvement, and organizational commitment. *Journal of Applied Psychology, 73,* 139-145.

Buchanan, B. (1974). Building organizational commitment: The socialization of managers in work organizations. *Administrative Science Quarterly, 19,* 533-546.

Buchholz, R. A. (1976). Measurement of beliefs. *Human Relations, 29,* 1177-1188.

Buchko, A. A. (1992). Employee ownership, attitudes, and turnover: An empirical assessment. *Human Relations, 45,* 711-733.

Buchko, A. A. (1993). The effects of employee ownership on employee attitudes: An integrated causal model and path analysis. *Journal of Management Studies, 30,* 633-657.

Buller, P. F. (1988). Successful partnerships: HR and strategic planning at eight top firms. *Organizational Dynamics, 17,* 27-43.

Buono, A. F., & Bowditch, J. L. (1989). *The human side of mergers and acquisitions.* San Francisco: Jossey-Bass.

Bycio, P., Hackett, R. D., & Allen, J. S. (1995). Further assessments of Bass's (1985) conceptualization of transactional and transformational leadership. *Journal of Applied Psychology, 80,* 468-478.

Byrne, D., & Clore, G. L. (1970). A reinforcement model of evaluative responses. *Personality, 1,* 103-127.

Caldwell, D. F., Chatman, J. A., & O'Reilly, C. A. (1990). Building organizational commitment: A multi-firm study. *Journal of Occupational Psychology, 63,* 245-261.

Cameron, K. S. (1994). Strategies for successful organizational downsizing. *Human Resource Management, 33,* 189-211.

Cartwright, S., & Cooper, C. L. (1993, August 29). If cultures don't fit, mergers may fail. *New York Times,* p. F9.

Cartwright, S., & Cooper, C. L. (1994). The human effects of mergers and acquisitions. In C. L. Cooper & D. M. Rousseau (Eds.), *Trends in organizational behavior* (Vol. 1, pp. 47-61). New York: John Wiley.

Cascio, W. F. (1982). *Costing human resources: The financial impact of behavior in organizations.* Boston: Kent.

Cascio, W. F. (1993). Downsizing: What do we know? What have we learned? *Academy of Management Executive, 7,* 95-104.

Cascio, W. F. (1995). Whither industrial and organizational psychology in a changing world of work? *American Psychologist, 50,* 928-939.

Caudron, S. (1993). How HR drives TQM. *Personnel Journal, 72,* 48B-48O.

Chao, G. T., O'Leary-Kelly, A. M., Wolf, S., Klein, H. J., & Gardner, P. D. (1994). Organizational socialization: Its content and consequences. *Journal of Applied Psychology, 79,* 730-743.

Cohen, A. (1991). Career stage as a moderator of the relationships between organizational commitment and its outcomes: A meta-analysis. *Journal of Occupational Psychology, 64,* 253-268.

Cohen, A. (1993a). Age and tenure in relation to organizational commitment: A meta-analysis. *Basic and Applied Social Psychology, 14,* 143-159.

Cohen, A. (1993b). On the discriminant validity of the Meyer and Allen (1984) measure of organizational commitment: How does it fit with the work commitment construct? In N. S. Bruning (Ed.), *Proceedings of the Annual Meeting of the Administrative Science Association of Canada: Organizational Behavior, 14,* 82-91.

Cohen, A., & Kirchmeyer, C. (1995). A multidimensional approach to the relation between organizational commitment and nonwork participation. *Journal of Vocational Behavior, 46,* 189-202.

Cohen, A., & Lowenberg, G. (1990). A re-examination of the side-bet theory as applied to organizational commitment: A meta-analysis. *Human Relations, 43,* 1015-1050.

Colarelli, S. M., Dean, R. A., & Konstans, C. (1987). Comparative effects of personal and situational influences on job outcomes of new professionals. *Journal of Applied Psychology, 72,* 558-566.

Cronbach, L. J., & Meehl, P. E. (1955). Construct validity in psychological tests. *Psychological Bulletin, 52,* 281-302.

Dalton, D. R., Krackhardt, D. M., & Porter, L. W. (1981). Functional turnover: An empirical assessment. *Journal of Applied Psychology, 66,* 716-721.

Darden, W. R., Hampton, R., & Howell, R. D. (1989). Career versus organizational commitment: Antecedents and consequences of retail salespeoples' commitment. *Journal of Retailing, 65,* 80-106.

Davy, J. A., Kinicki, A. J., & Scheck, C. L. (1991). Developing and testing a model of survivor responses to layoffs. *Journal of Vocational Behavior, 38,* 302-317.

Deci, E. L., & Ryan, R. M. (1991). Intrinsic motivation and self-determination in human behavior. In R. M. Steers & L. W. Porter (Eds.), *Motivation and work behavior* (44-57). New York: McGraw-Hill.

DeCotiis, T. A., & Summers, T. P. (1987). A path analysis of a model of the antecedents and consequences of organizational commitment. *Human Relations, 40,* 445-470.

Dunham, R. B., Grube, J. A., & Castaneda, M. B. (1994). Organizational commitment: The utility of an integrative definition. *Journal of Applied Psychology, 79,* 370-380.

Dyer, L., & Holder, G. W. (1988). Toward a strategic perspective of human resource management. In L. Dyer (Ed.), *Human resource management: Evolving roles and responsibilities* (pp. 1-46). Washington, DC: Bureau of National Affairs.

Edwards, J. R. (1991). Person-job fit: A conceptual integration, literature review, and methodological critique. In C. L. Cooper & I. T. Robertson (Eds.), *International review of industrial and organizational psychology* (Vol. 6, pp. 285-357). New York: John Wiley.

Edwards, J. R. (1993). Problems with the use of profile similarity indices in the study of congruence in organizational research. *Personnel Psychology, 46,* 641-665.

Edwards, J. R. (1994). The study of congruence in organizational behavior research: Critique and a proposed alternative. *Journal of Organizational Behavior and Human Decision Processes, 58,* 51-100.

Edwards, J. R., & Cooper, C. L. (1990). The person-environment fit approach to stress: Recurring problems and some suggested solutions. *Journal of Organizational Behavior, 11,* 293-308.

Eisenberger, R., Fasolo, P., & Davis-LaMastro, V. (1990). Perceived organizational support and employee diligence, commitment, and innovation. *Journal of Applied Psychology, 75,* 51-59.

Eisenberger, R., Huntington, R., Hutchison, S., & Sowa, D. (1986). Perceived organizational support. *Journal of Applied Psychology, 71,* 500-507.

Eisenhardt, K. M. (1985). Control: Organizational and economic approaches. *Management Science, 31,* 134-149.

Emshoff, J. R. (1994). How to increase employee loyalty while you downsize. *Business Horizons, 37,* 49-57.

The end of corporate loyalty. (1986, August 4). *Business Week,* pp. 42-49.

Facteau, J. D., Dobbins, G. H., Russell, J. E. A., Ladd, R. T., & Kudisch, J. D. (1995). The influence of general perceptions of the training environment on pretraining motivation and perceived training transfer. *Journal of Management, 21,* 1-25.

Farrell, D. (1983). Exit, voice, loyalty, and neglect as responses to job dissatisfaction: A multidimensional scaling study. *Academy of Management Journal, 26,* 596-607.

Farrell, D., & Rusbult, C. E. (1981). Exchange variables as predictors of job satisfaction, job commitment, and turnover: The impact of rewards, costs, alternatives, and investments. *Organizational Behavior and Human Performance, 27,* 78-95.

Feldman, D. C., & Leana, C. R. (1989). Managing layoffs: Experiences at the *Challenger* disaster site and the Pittsburgh Steel Mills. *Organizational Dynamics, 18,* 52-64.

Ferris, K. R., & Aranya, N. (1983). A comparison of two organizational commitment scales. *Personnel Psychology, 36,* 87-98.

Fletcher, C. (1991). Candidates' reactions to assessment centers and their outcomes: A longitudinal study. *Journal of Occupational Psychology, 64,* 117-127.

Florkowski, G. W., & Schuster, M. H. (1992). Support for profit sharing and organizational commitment: A path analysis. *Human Relations, 45,* 507-523.

Folger, R., & Konovsky, M. A. (1989). Effects of procedural and distributive justice on reactions to pay raise decisions. *Academy of Management Journal, 32,* 115-130.

For better or worse. (1987, January 12). *Business Week,* pp. 38-40.

Ford, R. C., & Perrewé, P. L. (1993, July-August). After the layoff: Closing the barn door before all the horses are gone. *Business Horizons, 36,* 34-40.

Fukami, C. V., & Larson, E. W. (1984). Commitment to company and union: Parallel models. *Journal of Applied Psychology, 69,* 367-371.

Fullagar, C., & Barling, J. (1991). Predictors and outcomes of different patterns of organizational and union loyalty. *Journal of Occupational Psychology, 64,* 129-143.

Fullagar, C. J. A., Gallagher, D. G., Gordon, M. E., & Clark, P. F. (1995). Impact of early socialization on union commitment and participation: A longitudinal study. *Journal of Applied Psychology, 80,* 147-157.

Gaertner, K. N., & Nollen, S. D. (1989). Career experiences, perceptions of employment practices, and psychological commitment to the organization. *Human Relations, 42,* 975-991.

Ganster, D. C., & Dwyer, D. J. (1995). The effects of understaffing on individual and group performance in professional and trade occupations. *Journal of Management, 21,* 175-190.

Gellatly, I. R. (1995). Individual and group determinants of employee absenteeism: Test of a causal model. *Journal of Organizational Behavior, 16,* 469-485.

Gleitman, H. (1981). *Psychology.* New York: Norton.

Goldberg, W. A., Greenberger, E., Koch-Jones, J., O'Neil, J., & Hamill, S. (1989). Attractiveness of child care and related employer-supported benefits and policies to married and single parents. *Child & Youth Care Quarterly, 18,* 23-37.

Gordon, M. E., & Ladd, R. T. (1990). Dual allegiance: Renewal, reconsideration, and recantation. *Personnel Psychology, 43,* 37-69.

Gordon, M. E., Philpot, J. W., Burt, R. E., Thompson, C. A., & Spiller, W. E. (1980). Commitment to the union: Development of a measure and an examination of its correlates. *Journal of Applied Psychology, 65,* 479-499.

Gouldner, A. W. (1960). The norm of reciprocity. *American Sociological Review, 25,* 165-167.

Graham, J. (1991). An essay on organizational citizenship behavior. *Employee Responsibilities and Rights Journal, 4,* 249-270.

Greenberg, J. (1994). Using socially fair treatment to promote acceptance of a worksite smoking ban. *Journal of Applied Psychology, 79,* 288-297.

Greenhalgh, L., & Jick, T. D. (1979). *The relationship between job insecurity and turnover and its differential effect on employee quality level.* Paper presented at the annual meeting of the Academy of Management, Atlanta, GA.

Greenhalgh, L., McKersie, R. B., & Gilkey, R. W. (1986). Rebalancing the workforce at IBM: A case study of redeployment and revitalization. *Organizational Dynamics, 14,* 30-47.

Greenhaus, J. H. (1971). An investigation of the role of career salience in vocational behavior. *Journal of Vocational Behavior, 1,* 209-216.

Gregersen, H. B. (1993). Multiple commitments at work and extra-role behavior during three stages of organizational tenure. *Journal of Business Research, 26,* 31-47.

Gregersen, H. B., & Black, J. S. (1992). Antecedents to commitment to a parent company and a foreign operation. *Academy of Management Journal, 35,* 65-90.

Griffin, R. W. (1991). Effects of work redesign on employee perceptions, attitudes, and behaviors: A long-term investigation. *Academy of Management Journal, 34,* 425-435.

Gross, A. B., & Fullagar, C. (1996, April). *Professional association participation: An application and extension of labor union models.* Paper presented at the annual meeting of the Society of Industrial and Organizational Psychology, San Diego, CA.

Grover, S. L., & Crooker, K. J. (1995). Who appreciates family-responsive human resource policies: The impact of family-friendly policies on the organizational attachment of parents and non-parents. *Personnel Psychology, 48,* 271-288.

Gunz, H. P., & Gunz, S. P. (1994). Professional/organizational commitment and job satisfaction for employed lawyers. *Human Relations, 47,* 801-828.

Guzzo, R. A., & Noonan, K. A. (1994). Human resource practices as communications and the psychological contract. *Human Resource Management, 33,* 447-462.

Guzzo, R. A., Noonan, K. A., & Elron, E. (1994). Expatriate managers and the psychological contract. *Journal of Applied Psychology, 79,* 617-626.

Hackett, R. D., Bycio, P., & Hausdorf, P. A. (1994). Further assessments of Meyer and Allen's (1991) three-component model of organizational commitment. *Journal of Applied Psychology, 79,* 15-23.

Hackman, J. R., & Oldham, G. R. (1980). *Work redesign.* Reading, MA: Addison-Wesley.

Hall, D. T., Schneider, B., & Nygren, H. T. (1970). Personal factors in organizational identification. *Administrative Science Quarterly, 15,* 176-190.

Hall, R. T. (1976). *Occupations and the social structure* (2nd ed.). Upper Saddle River, NJ: Prentice Hall.

Hammer, M., & Champy, J. (1993). *Reengineering the corporation: A manifesto for business revolution.* New York: HarperCollins.

Harris, S. G., Hirschfeld, R. R., Feild, H. S., & Mossholder, K. W. (1993). Psychological attachment: Relationships with job characteristics, attitudes, and preferences for newcomer development. *Group and Organization Management, 18,* 459-481.

Hirsch, P. (1987). *Pack your own parachute: How to survive mergers, takeovers, and other corporate disasters.* Reading, MA: Addison-Wesley.

Hirschman, A. O. (1970). *Exit, voice, and loyalty: Responses to decline in firms, organizations, and states.* Cambridge, MA: Harvard University Press.

Hofstede, G. (1980). *Culture's consequences: International differences in work-related values.* Beverly Hills, CA: Sage.

Hogan, E. A., & Overmyer-Day, L. (1994). The psychology of mergers and acquisitions. In C. L. Cooper & I. T. Robertson (Eds.), *International review of industrial and organizational psychology* (pp. 247-281). New York: John Wiley.

Hollenbeck, J. R., & Williams, C. R. (1986). Turnover functionality versus turnover frequency: A note on work attitudes and organizational effectiveness. *Journal of Applied Psychology, 71,* 606-611.

Hrebiniak, L. G., & Alutto, J. A. (1972). Personal and role-related factors in the development of organizational commitment. *Administrative Science Quarterly, 17,* 555-573.

Hunt, S. D., & Morgan, R. M. (1994). Organizational commitment: One of many commitments or key mediating construct? *Academy of Management Journal, 37,* 1568-1587.

Huselid, M. A. (1995). The impact of human resource management practices on turnover, productivity, and corporate financial performance. *Academy of Management Journal, 38*(3), 635-672.

Iles, P., Mabey, C., & Robertson, I. (1990). HRM practices and employee commitment: Possibilities, pitfalls, and paradoxes. *British Journal of Management, 1,* 147-157.

Iles, P. A., Robertson, I. T., & Rout, U. (1989). An investigation of assessment-based development centers. *Journal of Managerial Psychology, 4,* 11-16.

Ingram, T. N., Lee, K. S., & Skinner, S. (1989). An empirical assessment of salesperson motivation, commitment, and job outcomes. *Journal of Personal Selling and Sales Management, 9,* 25-33.

Irving, P. G., Coleman, D. F., & Cooper, C. L. (1996). *Further assessments of a three-component model of occupational commitment: Generalizability and differences across occupations.* Unpublished manuscript, University of New Brunswick, St. John, New Brunswick, Canada.

Irving, P. G., & Meyer, J. P. (1994). Reexamination of the met-expectations hypothesis: A longitudinal analysis. *Journal of Applied Psychology, 79,* 937-949.

Jackson, D. N. (1970). A sequential system for personality scale development. In C. D. Spielberger (Ed.), *Current topics in clinical and community psychology* (Vol. 2, pp. 61-96). San Diego, CA: Academic Press.

Jamal, M. (1990). Relationship of job stress and Type-A behavior to employees' job satisfaction, organizational commitment, psychosomatic health problems, and turnover motivation. *Human Relations, 43,* 727-738.

Jaros, S. T., Jermier, J. M., Koehler, J. W., & Sincich, T. (1993). Effects of continuance, affective, and moral commitment on the withdrawal process: An evaluation of eight structural equation models. *Academy of Management Journal, 36,* 951-995.

Jayne, M. (1994). *Family role identification as a source of gender differences in the relationship between parenthood and organizational commitment.* Unpublished doctoral dissertation, Tulane University, New Orleans, LA.

Jermier, J. M., & Berkes, L. J. (1979). Leader behavior in a police command bureaucracy: A closer look at the quasi-military model. *Administrative Science Quarterly, 24,* 1-23.

Johns, G. (1991). Substantive and methodological constraints on behavior and attitudes in organizational research. *Organizational Behavior and Human Performance, 2,* 309-328.

Johnston, G. P., & Snizek, W. (1991). Combining head and heart in complex organizations: A test of Etzioni's dual compliance structure hypothesis. *Human Relations, 44,* 1255-1272.

Johnston, M. W., Griffeth, R. W., Burton, S., & Carson, P. P. (1993). An exploratory investigation into the relationships between promotion and turnover: A quasi-experimental longitudinal study. *Journal of Management, 19,* 33-49.

Johnston, M. W., Parasuraman, A., Futrell, C. M., & Black, W. C. (1990). A longitudinal assessment of the impact of selected organizational influences on salespeoples' organizational commitment during early employment. *Journal of Marketing Research, 27,* 333-344.

Jones, G. R. (1986). Socialization tactics, self-efficacy, and newcomers' adjustments to organizations. *Academy of Management Journal, 29*(2), 262-279.

Kanter, R. M. (1968). Commitment and social organization: A study of commitment mechanisms in utopian communities. *American Sociological Review, 33,* 499-517.

Kanter, R. M. (1983). Frontiers for strategic human resource planning and management. *Human Resource Management, 22,* 9-21.

Kanungo, R. N. (1982). Measurement of job and work involvement. *Journal of Applied Psychology, 67,* 341-349.

Katz, D. (1964). The motivational basis of organizational behavior. *Behavioral Science, 9,* 131-146.

Kelloway, E. K., Barling, J., & Agar, S. (in press). Pre-employment predictors of union attitudes: The moderating role of parental identification. *Journal of Social Psychology.*

Kelloway, E. K., Catano, V. M., & Southwell, R. R. (1992). The construct validity of union commitment: Development and dimensionality of a shorter scale. *Journal of Occupational and Organizational Psychology, 65,* 197-211.

Kelloway, E. K., & Watts, L. (1994). Pre-employment predictors of union attitudes: Replication and extension. *Journal of Applied Psychology, 79,* 631-634.

Kelman, H. C. (1958). Compliance, identification, and internalization: Three processes of attitude change. *Journal of Conflict Resolution, 2,* 51-60.

Kerr, S., Von Glinow, M. A., & Schriesheim, J. (1977). Issues in the study of "professionals" in organizations: The case of scientists and engineers. *Organizational Behavior and Human Performance, 18,* 329-345.

Kiesler, C. A. (1971). *The psychology of commitment: Experiments linking behavior to belief.* San Diego, CA: Academic Press.

Kim, W. C., & Mauborgne, R. A. (1993). Procedural justice, attitudes, and subsidiary top management compliance with multinationals' corporate strategic decisions. *Academy of Management Journal, 36,* 502-528.

Kinicki, A. J., Carson, K. P., & Bohlander, G. W. (1992). Relationship between an organization's actual human resource efforts and employee attitudes. *Group & Organization Management, 17*(2), 135-152.

Kirchmeyer, C. (1992). Nonwork participation and work attitudes: A test of scarcity vs. expansion models of personal resources. *Human Relations, 45,* 775-795.

Klein, K. J. (1987). Employee stock ownership and employee attitudes: A test of three models. *Journal of Applied Psychology, 72,* 319-332.

Klein, K. J., & Hall, R. J. (1988). Correlates of employee satisfaction with stock ownership: Who likes an ESOP most? *Journal of Applied Psychology, 73,* 630-638.

Kline, C. J., & Peters, L. H. (1991). Behavioral commitment and tenure of new employees: A replication and extension. *Academy of Management Journal, 34,* 194-204.

Kobasa, S. C., Maddi, S. R., & Kahn, S. (1982). Hardiness and health: A prospective study. *Journal of Personality and Social Psychology, 42,* 168-177.

Konovsky, M. A., & Cropanzano, R. (1991). Perceived fairness of employee drug testing as a predictor of employee attitudes and job performance. *Journal of Applied Psychology, 76,* 698-707.

Koys, D. J. (1988). Human resource management and a culture of respect: Effects on employees' organizational commitment. *Employee Responsibilities and Rights Journal, 1,* 57-68.

Koys, D. J. (1991). Fairness, legal compliance, and organizational commitment. *Employee Responsibilities and Rights Journal, 4,* 283-291.

Lawler, E. E. (1986). *High involvement management.* San Francisco: Jossey-Bass.

Lawler, E. J. (1992). Affective attachment to nested groups: A choice process theory. *American Sociological Review, 57,* 327-339.

Lee, K. B. (1992). *A study of affective, continuance, and normative commitment to the organization.* Unpublished master's thesis, Sung Kyun Kwan University, Seoul, Korea.

Lee, T. W., Ashford, S. J., Walsh, J. P., & Mowday, R. T. (1992). Commitment propensity, organizational commitment, and voluntary turnover: A longitudinal study of organizational entry processes. *Journal of Management, 18,* 15-32.

Leonard, B. (1992, June). HR policies ensure the mirage won't vanish. *HR Magazine,* 85-91.

Leong, S. M., Randall, D. M., & Cote, J. A. (1994). Exploring the organizational commitment-performance linkage in marketing: A study of life insurance salespeople. *Journal of Business Research, 29,* 57-63.

Leventhal, G. S. (1980). What should be done with equity theory? In K. J. Gergen, M. S. Greenberg, & R. H. Willis (Eds.), *Social exchange: Advances in theory and research* (pp. 27-55). New York: Plenum.

Lincoln, J. R. (1989). Employee work attitudes and management practice in the U.S. and Japan: Evidence from a large comparative survey. *California Management Review, 32,* 89-106.

Lind, E. A., & Tyler, T. R. (1988). *The social psychology of procedural justice.* New York: Plenum.

Lodahl, T. M., & Kejner, M. (1965). The definition and measurement of job involvement. *Journal of Applied Psychology, 49,* 24-33.

Lowe, R. H., & Vodanovich, S. J. (1995). A field study of distributive and procedural justice as predictors of satisfaction and organizational commitment. *Journal of Business and Psychology, 10,* 99-114.

Luthans, F., McCaul, H. S., & Dodd, N. G. (1985). Organizational commitment: A comparison of American, Japanese, and Korean employees. *Academy of Management Journal, 28,* 213-219.

MacDuffie, J. P. (1995). Human resource bundles and manufacturing performance: Organizational logic and flexible production systems in the world auto industry. *Industrial and Labor Relations Review, 48,* 197-221.

MacNeil, I. R. (1985). Relational contracts: What we do and do not know. *Wisconsin Law Review,* 483-525.

Major, D. A., Kozlowski, S. W. J., Chao, G. T., & Gardner, P. D. (1995). A longitudinal investigation of newcomer expectations, early socialization outcomes, and the moderating effects of role development factors. *Journal of Applied Psychology, 80,* 418-431.

Marsden, P. V., Kalleberg, A. L., & Cook, C. R. (1993). Gender differences in organizational commitment: Influences of work positions and family roles. *Work and Occupations, 20,* 368-390.

Marsh, R. M., & Mannari, H. (1977). Organizational commitment and turnover: A predictive study. *Administrative Science Quarterly, 22,* 57-75.

Martin, J. E., & Berthiaume, R. D. (1993). Stress and the union steward's role. *Journal of Organizational Behavior, 14,* 433-446.

Mathieu, J. E. (1988). A causal model of organizational commitment in a military training environment. *Journal of Vocational Behavior, 32,* 321-335.

Mathieu, J. E., & Farr, J. L. (1991). Further evidence for the discriminant validity of measures of organizational commitment, job involvement, and job satisfaction. *Journal of Applied Psychology, 76,* 127-133.

Mathieu, J. E., & Hamel, K. (1989). A causal model of the antecedents of organizational commitment among professionals and nonprofessionals. *Journal of Vocational Behavior, 34,* 299-317.

Mathieu, J. E., & Zajac, D. (1990). A review and meta-analysis of the antecedents, correlates, and consequences of organizational commitment. *Psychological Bulletin, 108,* 171-194.

Mayer, R. C., & Schoorman, F. D. (1992). Predicting participation and production outcomes through a two-dimensional model of organizational commitment. *Academy of Management Journal, 35,* 671-684.

McEvoy, G. M., & Cascio, W. F. (1985). Strategies for reducing employee turnover: A meta-analysis. *Journal of Applied Psychology, 70,* 342-353.

McGee, G. W., & Ford, R. C. (1987). Two (or more?) dimensions of organizational commitment: Reexamination of the Affective and Continuance Commitment Scales. *Journal of Applied Psychology, 72,* 638-642.

Meglino, B. M., Ravlin, E. C., & Adkins, C. L. (1989). A work values approach to corporate culture: A field test of the value congruence process and its relationship to individual outcomes. *Journal of Applied Psychology, 74,* 424-432.

Mellor, S. (1992). The influence of layoff severity on postlayoff union commitment among survivors: The moderating effect of the perceived legitimacy of a layoff account. *Personnel Psychology, 45,* 579-600.

Meyer, J. P., & Allen, N. J. (1984). Testing the "side-bet theory" of organizational commitment: Some methodological considerations. *Journal of Applied Psychology, 69,* 372-378.

Meyer, J. P., & Allen, N. J. (1986, June). *Development and consequences of three components of organizational commitment.* Paper presented at the annual meeting of the Administrative Sciences Association of Canada, Whistler, British Columbia.

Meyer, J. P., & Allen, N. J. (1991). A three-component conceptualization of organizational commitment. *Human Resource Management Review, 1,* 61-89.

Meyer, J. P., & Allen, N. J. (1995, May). *Work characteristic and work attitude relations: Moderating effect of attributions.* Paper presented at the annual meeting of the Society of Industrial and Organizational Psychology, Orlando, FL.

Meyer, J. P., Allen, N. J., & Gellatly, I. R. (1990). Affective and continuance commitment to the organization: Evaluation of measures and analysis of concurrent and time-lagged relations. *Journal of Applied Psychology, 75,* 710-720.

Meyer, J. P., Allen, N. J., & Smith, C. A. (1993). Commitment to organizations and occupations: Extension and test of a three-component conceptualization. *Journal of Applied Psychology, 78,* 538-551.

Meyer, J. P., Bobocel, D. R., & Allen, N. J. (1991). Development of organizational commitment during the first year of employment: A longitudinal study of pre- and post-entry influences. *Journal of Management, 17,* 717-733.

Meyer, J. P., & Gardner, R. C. (1994, March). *Assessment of change in organizational commitment during the first year of employment: An application of confirmatory factor analysis.* Paper presented at the Academy of Management, Research Methods Division, Conference on Causal Modelling, West Lafayette, IN.

Meyer, J. P., Irving, G. P., & Allen, N. J. (in press). Test of the moderating effect of work values on the relations between early work experiences and organizational commitment. *Journal of Organizational Behavior.*

Meyer, J. P., Paunonen, S. V., Gellatly, I. H., Goffin, R. D., & Jackson, D. N. (1989). Organizational commitment and job performance: It's the nature of the commitment that counts. *Journal of Applied Psychology, 74,* 152-156.

Mignerey, J. T., Rubin, R. B., & Gorden, W. I. (1995). Organizational entry: An investigation of newcomer communication behavior and uncertainty. *Communication Research, 22,* 54-85.

Miles, R. E., & Snow, C. C. (1984). Designing strategic human resource systems. *Organizational Dynamics, 31,* 36-52.

Mirels, H. L., & Garrett, J. B. (1971). The Protestant ethic as a personality variable. *Journal of Consulting and Clinical Psychology, 36,* 40-44.

Mone, M. A. (1994). Relationships between self-concepts, aspirations, emotional responses, and intent to leave a downsizing organization. *Human Resource Management, 33,* 281-298.

Moorman, R. H., Niehoff, B. P., & Organ, D. W. (1993). Treating employees fairly and organizational citizenship behavior: Sorting the effects of job satisfaction, organizational commitment, and procedural justice. *Employee Responsibilities and Rights Journal, 6,* 209-225.

Morris, J. H., & Steers, R. M. (1980). Structural influences on organizational commitment. *Journal of Vocational Behavior, 17,* 50-57.

Morrison, E. W. (1993). Longitudinal study of the effects of information seeking on newcomer socialization. *Journal of Applied Psychology, 78,* 173-183.

Morrison, E. W. (1994). Role definitions and organizational citizenship behavior: The importance of the employee's perspective. *Academy of Management Journal, 37,* 1543-1567.

Morrow, P. C. (1983). Concept redundancy in organizational research: The case of work commitment. *Academy of Management Review, 8,* 486-500.

Morrow, P. C. (1993). *The theory and measurement of work commitment.* Greenwich, CT: JAI.

Morrow, P. C., & McElroy, J. C. (1986). On assessing measures of work commitment. *Journal of Occupational Behavior, 7,* 139-145.

Morrow, P. C., & McElroy, J. C. (1993). Introduction: Understanding and managing loyalty in a multi-commitment world. *Journal of Business Research, 26,* 1-2.

Mottaz, C. J. (1988). Determinants of organizational commitment. *Human Relations, 41,* 467-482.

Mowday, R. T., Porter, L. W., & Dubin, R. (1974). Unit performance, situational factors, and employee attitudes. *Organizational Behavior and Human Performance, 12,* 231-248.

Mowday, R. T., Porter, L. W., & Steers, R. (1982). *Organizational linkages: The psychology of commitment, absenteeism, and turnover.* San Diego, CA: Academic Press.

Mowday, R. T., Steers, R. M., & Porter, L. W. (1979). The measurement of organizational commitment. *Journal of Vocational Behavior, 14,* 224-247.

Mueller, C. W., Wallace, J. E., & Price, J. L. (1992). Employee commitment: Resolving some issues. *Work and Occupations, 19,* 211-236.

Munene, J. C. (1995). "Not on seat": An investigation of some correlates of organizational citizenship behavior in Nigeria. *Applied Psychology: An International Review, 44,* 111-222.

Near, J. P. (1989). Organizational commitment among Japanese and U.S. workers. *Organizational Studies, 10,* 281-300.

Newman, J. M., & Krzystofiak, F. J. (1993). Changes in employee attitudes after an acquisition: A longitudinal analysis. *Group and Organization Management, 18,* 390-410.

Niehoff, B. P., & Moorman, R. H. (1993). Justice as a mediator of the relationship between methods of monitoring and organizational citizenship behavior. *Academy of Management Journal, 36,* 527-556.

Nouri, H. (1994). Using organizational commitment and job involvement to predict budgetary slack: A research note. *Accounting Organization and Society, 19,* 289-295.

Ogilvie, J. R. (1986). The role of human resource management practices in predicting organizational commitment. *Group & Organization Studies, 11,* 335-359.

O'Neill, H. M., & Lenn, D. J. (1995). Voices of survivors: Words that downsizing CEOs should hear. *Academy of Management Executive, 9,* 23-34.

O'Reilly, C. A., & Caldwell, D. F. (1981). The commitment and job tenure of new employees: Some evidence of postdecisional justification. *Administrative Science Quarterly, 26,* 597-616.

O'Reilly, C. A., & Chatman, J. (1986). Organizational commitment and psychological attachment: The effects of compliance, identification, and internalization on prosocial behavior. *Journal of Applied Psychology, 71,* 492-499.

O'Reilly, C. A., Chatman, J., & Caldwell, D. F. (1991). People and organizational culture: A profile comparison approach to assessing person-organization fit. *Academy of Management Journal, 34,* 487-516.

Organ, D. W. (1988). *Organizational citizenship behavior.* Lexington, MA: Lexington Books.

Organ, D. W., & Ryan, K. (1995). A meta-analytic review of attitudinal and dispositional predictors of organizational citizenship behavior. *Personnel Psychology, 48,* 775-802.

Osterman, P. (1987). Choice of employment systems in internal labor markets. *Industrial Relations, 26,* 46-67.

Ostroff, C. (1992). The relationship between satisfaction, attitudes, and performance: An organizational level analysis. *Journal of Applied Psychology, 77,* 963-974.

Ostroff, C. (1993). Comparing correlations based on individual-level and aggregated data. *Journal of Applied Psychology, 78,* 569-582.

Ostroff, C., & Kozlowski, S. W. J. (1992). Organizational socialization as a learning process: The role of information acquisition. *Personnel Psychology, 45,* 849-874.

Pascale, R. (1985). The paradox of "corporate culture": Reconciling ourselves to socialization. *California Management Review, 27,* 26-41.

Pearce, J. L. (1993). Toward an organizational behavior of contract laborers: Their psychological involvement and effects on employee coworkers. *Academy of Management Journal, 36,* 1082-1096.

Penley, L. E., & Gould, S. (1988). Etzioni's model of organizational involvement: A perspective for understanding commitment to organizations. *Journal of Organizational Behavior, 9,* 43-59.

Pierce, J. L., & Dunham, R. B. (1987). Organizational commitment: Pre-employment propensity and initial work experiences. *Journal of Management, 13,* 163-178.

Pierce, J. L., & Furo, C. A. (1990). Employee ownership: Implications for management. *Organizational Dynamics, 18,* 32-43.

Premack, S. L., & Wanous, J. P. (1985). A meta-analysis of realistic job preview experiments. *Journal of Applied Psychology, 70,* 706-719.

A question of loyalty. (1991, September 23). *Newsweek,* p. 8.

Raelin, J. A. (1989). An anatomy of autonomy: Managing professionals. *Academy of Management Executive, 3,* 216-228.

Randall, D. M. (1987). Commitment and the organization: The organization man revisited. *Academy of Management Review, 12,* 460-471.

Randall, D. M. (1990). The consequences of organizational commitment: Methodological investigation. *Journal of Organizational Behavior, 11,* 361-378.

Randall, D. M. (1993). Cross-cultural research on organizational commitment: A review and application of Hofstede's value survey module. *Journal of Business Research, 26,* 91-110.

Randall, D. M., & Cote, J. A. (1991). Interrelationships of work commitment constructs. *Work and Occupations, 18,* 194-211.

Randall, D. M., Fedor, D. B., & Longenecker, C. O. (1990). The behavioral expression of organizational commitment. *Journal of Vocational Behavior, 36,* 210-224.

Reichers, A. E. (1985). A review and reconceptualization of organizational commitment. *Academy of Management Review, 10,* 465-476.

Reichers, A. E. (1986). Conflict and organizational commitments. *Journal of Applied Psychology, 71,* 508-514.

Reichheld, F. F. (1996). *The loyalty effect.* Boston: Harvard Business School Press.

Reilly, N. P., & Orsak, C. L. (1991). A career stage analysis of career and organizational commitment in nursing. *Journal of Vocational Behavior, 39,* 311-330.

Rhodes, S. R., & Steers, R. M. (1981). Conventional vs. worker-owned organizations. *Human Relations, 12,* 1013-1035.

Ritzer, G., & Trice, H. M. (1969). An empirical study of Howard Becker's side-bet theory. *Social Forces, 47,* 475-479.

Robertson, I. T., Iles, P. A., Gratton, L., & Sharpley, D. (1991). The impact of personnel selection and assessment methods on candidates. *Human Relations, 44,* 963-982.

Robinson, S. L., Kraatz, M. S., & Rousseau, D. M. (1994). Changing obligations and the psychological contract: A longitudinal study. *Academy of Management Journal, 37,* 137-152.

Rohlen, T. P. (1974). *For harmony and strength: Japanese white-collar organization in anthropological perspective.* Berkeley: University of California Press.

Romzek, B. S. (1989). Personal consequences of employee commitment. *Academy of Management Journal, 32,* 649-661.

Rousseau, D. M. (1989). Psychological and implicit contracts in organizations. *Employee Rights and Responsibilities Journal, 2,* 121-139.

Rousseau, D. M. (1995). *Promises in action: Psychological contracts in organizations.* Newbury Park, CA: Sage.

Rousseau, D. M., & Wade-Benzoni, K. A. (1995). Changing individual-organization attachments. In A. Howard (Ed.), *The changing nature of work* (290-322). San Francisco: Jossey-Bass.

Sadri, G., Cooper, C., & Allison, T. (1989, August). A post office initiative to stamp out stress. *Personnel Management,* 40-45.

Sager, J. K., & Johnston, M. W. (1989). Antecedents and outcomes of organizational commitment: A study of salespeople. *Journal of Personal Selling and Sales Management, 9,* 30-41.

Saks, A. M. (1995). Longitudinal field investigation of the moderating and mediating effects of self-efficacy on the relationship between training and newcomer adjustment. *Journal of Applied Psychology, 80,* 211-225.

Salancik, G. (1977a). Commitment and the control of organizational behavior and belief. In B. Staw & G. Salancik (Eds.), *New directions in organizational behavior* (pp. 1-54). Chicago: St. Clair.

Salancik, G. (1977b). Commitment is too easy! *Organizational Dynamics, 6,* 62-80.

Sanchez, J. I., Korbin, W. P., & Viscarra, D. M. (1995). Corporate support in the aftermath of a natural disaster: Effects on employee strains. *Academy of Management Journal, 38,* 504-521.

Schaubroeck, J., & Ganster, D. C. (1991). Beyond the call of duty: A field study of extra-role behavior in voluntary organizations. *Human Relations, 44,* 569-582.

Schaubroeck, J., May, D. R., & Brown, F. W. (1994). Procedural justice explanations and employee reactions to economic hardship: A field experiment. *Journal of Applied Psychology, 79,* 455-460.

Schein, E. H. (1980). *Organizational psychology.* Upper Saddle River, NJ: Prentice Hall.

Scholl, R. W. (1981). Differentiating commitment from expectancy as a motivating force. *Academy of Management Review, 6,* 589-599.

Schuler, R. S., & Jackson, S. E. (1987). Linking competitive strategies with human resource management practices. *Academy of Management Executive, 1,* 207-219.

Schwab, D. P. (1980). Construct validity in organizational behavior. *Research in Organizational Behavior, 2,* 3-43.

Schwarzwald, J., Koslowsky, M., & Shalit, B. (1992). A field study of employees' attitudes and behaviors after promotion decisions. *Journal of Applied Psychology, 77,* 511-514.

Schweiger, D. M., & DeNisi, A. S. (1991). Communication with employees following a merger: A longitudinal field experiment. *Academy of Management Journal, 34,* 110-135.

Seligman, M. E. P. (1975). *Helplessness: On depression, development, and death.* New York: Freeman.

Sheldon, M. E. (1971). Investments and involvements as mechanisms producing commitment to the organization. *Administrative Science Quarterly, 16,* 143-150.

Shim, W., & Steers, R. M. (1994). *Mediating influences on the employee commitment-job performance relationship.* Unpublished manuscript.

Shore, L. M., & Tetrick, L. E. (1991). A construct validity study of the Survey of Perceived Organizational Support. *Journal of Applied Psychology, 76,* 637-643.

Shore, L. M., & Tetrick, L. E. (1994). The psychological contract as an exploratory framework in the employment relationship. In C. L. Cooper & D. M. Rousseau (Eds.), *Trends in organizational behavior* (Vol. 1, pp. 91-109). New York: John Wiley.

Shore, L. M., & Wayne, S. J. (1993). Commitment and employee behavior: Comparison of affective and continuance commitment with perceived organizational support. *Journal of Applied Psychology, 78,* 774-780.

Snell, S. A., & Youndt, M. A. (1995). Human resource management and firm performance: Testing a contingency model of executive controls. *Journal of Management, 21,* 711-737.

Somers, M. J. (1993). A test of the relationship between affective and continuance commitment using non-recursive models. *Journal of Occupational and Organizational Psychology, 66,* 185-192.

Somers, M. J. (1995). Organizational commitment, turnover, and absenteeism: An examination of direct and interaction effects. *Journal of Organizational Behavior, 16,* 49-58.

Somers, M. J., & Casal, J. C. (1994). Organizational commitment and whistle-blowing. *Group and Organization Management, 19,* 270-284.

Speechley, M., Noh, S., & Beggs, C. (1993). Examining the psychometric properties of a scale on a smallish sample: An example using an occupational commitment scale. *Canadian Journal of Rehabilitation, 7,* 90-93.

Staw, B. M. (1974). Attitudinal and behavioral consequences of changing a major organizational reward: A natural field experiment. *Journal of Personality and Social Psychology, 6,* 742-751.

Staw, B. M. (1977, August). *Two sides of commitment.* Paper presented at the annual meeting of the Academy of Management, Orlando, FL.

Staw, B. M., & Ross, J. (1987). Behavior in escalation situations: Antecedents, prototypes, and solutions. In L. L. Cummings & B. M. Staw (Eds.), *Research in organizational behavior* (Vol. 7, pp. 297-332). Greenwich, CT: JAI.

Steers, R. M. (1977). Antecedents and outcomes of organizational commitment. *Administrative Science Quarterly, 22,* 46-56.

Sweeney, P. D., & McFarlin, D. B. (1993). Workers' evaluations of the "ends" and the "means": An examination of four models of distributive and procedural justice. *Organizational Behavior and Human Decision Processes, 55,* 23-40.

Tajfel, H. (1982). *Social identity and intergroup relations.* Cambridge, UK: Cambridge University Press.

Tannenbaum, S. I., Mathieu, J. E., Salas, E., & Cannon-Bowers, J. A. (1991). Meeting trainees' expectations: The influence of training fulfillment on the development of commitment, self-efficacy, and motivation. *Journal of Applied Psychology, 76,* 759-769.

Tett, R. P., & Meyer, J. P. (1993). Job satisfaction, organizational commitment, turnover intention, and turnover: Path analyses based on meta-analytic findings. *Personnel Psychology, 46,* 259-293.

Tucker, J., Nock, S. L., & Toscano, D. J. (1989). Employee ownership and perceptions at work. *Work and Occupations, 16,* 26-42.

Tyler, T. R., & Bies, R. J. (1990). Beyond formal procedures: The interpersonal context of procedural justice. In J. S. Carroll (Ed.), *Applied social psychology and organizational settings.* Hillsdale, NJ: Lawrence Erlbaum.

Vancouver, J. B., Millsap, R. E., & Peters, P. A. (1994). Multilevel analysis of organizational goal congruence. *Journal of Applied Psychology, 79,* 666-679.

Vancouver, J. B., & Schmitt, N. W. (1991). An exploratory examination of person-organization fit: Organizational goal congruence. *Personnel Psychology, 44,* 333-352.

Vandenberg, R. J., & Self, R. M. (1993). Assessing newcomers' changing commitments to the organization during the first 6 months of work. *Journal of Applied Psychology, 78,* 557-568.

Vandenberg, R. J., Self, R. M., & Seo, J. H. (1994). A critical examination of the internalization, identification, and compliance commitment measures. *Journal of Management, 20,* 123-140.

Vandenberghe, C. (1996). Assessing organizational commitment in a Belgian context: Evidence for the three-dimensional model. *Applied Psychology: An International Review, 45,* 371-386.

Van Maanen, J., & Schein, E. H. (1979). Toward a theory of organizational socialization. *Research in Organizational Behavior, 1,* 209-264.

Vardi, Y., Wiener, Y., & Popper, M. (1989). The value content of organizational mission as a factor in the commitment of members. *Psychological Reports, 65,* 27-34.

Wahn, J. (1993). Organizational dependence and the likelihood of complying with organizational pressures to behave unethically. *Journal of Business Ethics, 12,* 245-251.

Walker, J. M., & Lawler, J. J. (1979). Dual unions and political processes in organizations. *Industrial Relations, 18,* 32-43.

Wallace, J. E. (1993). Professional and organizational commitment: Compatible or incompatible? *Journal of Vocational Behavior, 42,* 333-349.

Walton, R. E. (1985). Toward a strategy of eliciting employee commitment based on policies of mutuality. In R. E. Walton & P. R. Lawrence (Eds.), *Human resource management trends and challenges.* Boston: Harvard Business School.

Wanous, J. P. (1980). *Organizational entry.* Reading, MA: Addison-Wesley.

Wanous, J. P. (1992). *Organizational entry: Recruitment, selection, orientation, and socialization of newcomers* (2nd ed.). Reading, MA: Addison-Wesley.

Wanous, J. P., & Colella, A. (1989). Organizational entry research: Current status and future directions. *Research in Personnel and Human Resources Management, 7,* 59-120.

Wanous, J. P., Poland, T. D., Premack, S. L., & Davis, K. S. (1992). The effects of met expectations on newcomer attitudes and behaviors: A review and meta-analysis. *Journal of Applied Psychology, 77,* 288-297.

Wetzel, K. W., & Gallagher, D. G. (1990). A comparative analysis of organizational commitment among workers in the cooperative and private sectors. *Economic and Industrial Democracy, 11,* 93-109.

Whitener, E. M., & Walz, P. M. (1993). Exchange theory determinants of affective and continuance commitment and turnover. *Journal of Vocational Behavior, 42,* 265-281.

Whyte, W. (1956). *The organization man.* Garden City, NY: Doubleday.

Wiener, Y. (1982). Commitment in organizations: A normative view. *Academy of Management Review, 7,* 418-428.

Wiener, Y., & Gechman, A. S. (1977). Commitment: A behavioral approach to job involvement. *Journal of Vocational Behavior, 10,* 47-52.

Williams, L. J., & Anderson, S. E. (1991). Job satisfaction and organizational commitment as predictors of organizational citizenship and in-role behaviors. *Journal of Management, 17,* 601-617.

Williams, M. L., Podsakoff, P. M., & Huber, V. (1992). Effects of group-level and individual-level variation in leader behaviors on subordinate attitudes and performance. *Journal of Occupational Psychology, 65,* 115-129.

Withey, M. (1988). Antecedents of value based and economic organizational commitment. *Proceedings of the Annual Meeting of the Administrative Sciences Association of Canada—Organizational Behavior Division, 9,* 124-133.

Withey, M. J. (1990). *Students' commitment to their academic program: Antecedents and consequences.* Paper presented at the annual meeting of the Administrative Sciences Association of Canada, Whistler, British Columbia.

Workplace of the future: A report of the Conference on the Future of the American Workplace. (1993). New York: U.S. Departments of Commerce and Labor.

Wright, P. M., & McMahan, G. C. (1992). Theoretical perspectives for strategic human resource management. *Journal of Management, 18,* 295-320.

Yoon, J., Baker, M. R., & Ko, J. W. (1994). Interpersonal attachment and organizational commitment: Subgroup hypothesis revisited. *Human Relations, 47,* 329-351.

Zaccaro, S. J., & Dobbins, G. H. (1989). Contrasting group and organizational commitment: Evidence for differences among multilevel attachments. *Journal of Organizational Behavior, 10,* 267-273.

Author Index

Subject Index

About the Authors

John P. Meyer received his Ph.D. in 1978 from the University of Western Ontario, where he is Professor and Director of the Industrial and Organizational Psychology program. In addition to his work on commitment, he has conducted research in the areas of work motivation, organizational justice, conflict management, personality and job performance, and performance appraisal. His research has been published in leading journals in the fields of I/O psychology (e.g., *Journal of Applied Psychology, Journal of Occupational Psychology*) and management (e.g., *Academy of Management Journal, Journal of Management*). He is currently involved in research to examine the cross-cultural generalizability of the commitment model he developed with Natalie Allen.

Natalie J. Allen received her Ph.D. in 1985 from the University of Western Ontario, where she is Associate Professor in the Department of Psychology. Prior to joining the Psychology Department, she was Director of the Center for Administrative and Information Studies, a multidisciplinary research and teaching unit at Western. Although much of her research has focused on commitment in the workplace, other research interests include cross-cultural issues within organizational behavior and the psychology of work teams. Her work has appeared in the *Journal of Applied Psychology, Evaluation and Program Planning, Journal of Vocational Behavior,* and *Academy of Management Journal.*